ELDAR

by Phil Kelly

PRODUCED BY GAMES WORKSHOP

ISBN: 1-84154-791-3   Games Workshop web site: www.games-workshop.com   Product Code: 60 03 01 04 003

INTRODUCTION

Eldar are highly advanced and deadly aliens, feared across the galaxy, even as their race is slowly dying. Codex: Eldar is the definitive guide to collecting, painting and playing with an Eldar army for the Warhammer 40,000 game.

THE WARHAMMER 40,000 GAME

The Warhammer 40,000 rulebook contains the rules you need to fight battles with your Citadel miniatures in the war-torn universe of the 41st millennium. Every army has its own codex book that works with these rules and allows you to turn your collection of miniatures into an army organised and ready for battle. This codex describes the enigmatic alien Eldar, details the army, and displays the miniatures you can collect.

WHY COLLECT AN ELDAR ARMY?

A typical Eldar force consists of specialist units that each excel at one of the arts of war. They are supported by extremely powerful psykers, and sleek Eldar skimmers bristling with a daunting array of heavy weapons. All this excellence is balanced out by having comparatively few troops, which is why Eldar commanders must ensure they get the most out of each unit. If all the elements of the Eldar army work in concert, you will find they are practically unstoppable.

The Eldar are an immensely rewarding army to play, with striking colour schemes and stunning centrepiece models. Used skilfully, the Eldar can destroy an enemy force in short order and look stylish while doing it!

HOW THIS BOOK WORKS

This codex is split into four main sections that deal with different aspects of the army:

The Eldar

The first section introduces the ancient Eldar race and their part in the Warhammer 40,000 universe. It includes history from the catastrophic times of the Fall, a guide to the immense spacefaring craftworlds and their methods of war, as well as information on the Eldar's arcane myths and strange technology.

Forces of the Eldar

Each and every character, troop type and vehicle in the Eldar army is examined in the second section. You will find a full description, alongside complete rules and details of any unique powers they possess or specialist wargear they carry into battle.

Eldar Army List

The army list takes all of the troops presented in the previous section and arranges them so you can choose a force for your games. The army list categorises the units you can pick into HQ, Troops, Elites, Fast Attack and Heavy Support choices. Each troop type also has a points value to help you pit your force against an opponent's in a game of Warhammer 40,000.

The Eldar Warhost

In the final section you will see photographs of the range of Citadel miniatures available for the Eldar army, gloriously painted by Games Workshop's famous 'Eavy Metal team. Colour schemes for the different craftworlds and Aspect Warriors can be found in this section.

FIND OUT MORE

While Codex: Eldar contains everything you need to play a game with your army, there are always more tactics to use, different battles to fight and painting ideas to try out. The monthly magazine White Dwarf contains articles about all aspects of the Warhammer 40,000 game and hobby, and you can find articles specific to the Eldar on our web site:

www.games-workshop.com

THE ELDAR

Lost in the vastness of space, the craftworlds float in utter isolation like scattered jewels upon a pall of velvet. No star-shine illuminates their sleek towers. Distant from the warmth of sun or planet, their domes stare into the darkness of empty space. Inner lights glisten like phosphorus through semi-transparent surfaces. Within live the survivors of a civilisation abandoned aeons ago amidst terrifying destruction. These are the Eldar, a race that is all but extinct, the last remnants of a people whose mere dreams once overturned worlds and quenched suns.

THE ELDAR RACE

The Eldar have a long and complex spacefaring history, so long in fact that little is known for certain about the course of their early physical evolution and planet-bound existence. Their homeworlds were destroyed during the catastrophic collapse of the Eldar civilisation known as the Fall. The remnants of their people, who survived that dark time by fleeing upon great spaceships called craftworlds, preserve echoes of their racial history in the form of traditional stories, songs and dance. The craftworlds contain the last remnant of the breathtaking architecture and legendary works of art that typified the Eldar empire.

Eldar are extremely long lived by Human standards, commonly surviving for over a thousand years before old age overtakes them. They also live at a pace and pitch of intensity many times greater than even the most exceptional Humans. An Eldar's heart beats almost twice as fast as a Man's, his mind processes thoughts and emotions with baffling speed, and his physical reactions are almost too fast for the Human eye to follow.

At first glance the Eldar are physically similar to Humans, although on closer examination there are several differences. They have longer, cleaner limbs and elegant features with penetrating, slanted eyes. Their ears are pointed, and their fine, alabaster skin is without blemish. The most fundamental difference can be seen when the Eldar move, for they radiate an inhuman elegance. This is evident in the sinuous grace with which they fight and the dexterity with which they wield their weaponry.

All Eldar can manipulate mental energies to a degree. Their complex technology is based upon psychotropic engineering, the manipulation of matter using psychic energy. But such raw mental power has its price. The Eldar mind is far more inclined towards extremes than that of a Human. To an Eldar, all of life's experiences are available to a heightened degree: the intellectual rewards of study, the exhilaration of battle, and every imaginable pleasure or sensation. This potential for joy is paralleled by an equal capacity to feel despair, anger and even hatred.

No creature, not even an Eldar, can taste such rich fruits in an uncontrolled or undisciplined way without consequence. For an Eldar to yield absolutely to his desires would destroy him. Such was the fate of the ancient Eldar, whose depravities brought about the birth of a vicious and obscene god, and consequently the fall of the Eldar race itself.

THE FALL OF THE ELDAR

O ver a million years ago, when their civilisation was at its height, the Eldar held dominion over a large portion of the galaxy. Their worlds were places of great peace and beauty, each one a utopia of personal contentment and cultural achievement. All this was to end in the cataclysm known simply as the Fall. The prehistory of the Eldar is lost to time, remembered only in quasi-historical mythic cycles. Whether these tales are a mere echo of actual history is unknown, but what follows is the story of the Fall as accepted by the Eldar of the craftworlds.

THE CHILDREN OF THE STARS

The Eldar were a proud and arrogant people, confident in their superiority and justifiably dismissive of alien barbarians. Their technological and cultural achievements excelled those of all other races, and in their hubris none amongst them doubted that this state of affairs would continue indefinitely. In many ways the Eldar had good reason for such conceit, for no other race had posed a serious threat to their wealth and stability for countless millennia. The doom of the Eldar, when it came, took a form far more subtle and dangerous than that of an invasion.

In those ancient times there were no craftworlds and the rigid constraints of the Eldar path did not exist. On hundreds of paradise worlds seeded across the stars, all Eldar pursued their inclinations according to their own will, indulging every whim and investigating every curiosity. They created many beautiful things and learned much about the universe that has since been forgotten. When their spirits eventually left their mortal bodies they dissolved peacefully back into the Warp to be reborn again; for the Warp did not have such a thirst for Eldar souls as it does today.

DECADENCE AND EXILE

Slowly but surely, the worm of pride began to eat away at the Eldar race. They thought all secrets theirs to uncover, all pleasures theirs to partake. Heedlessly they plundered the precious resources of their marvellous minds. The Eldar had long outgrown the need for labour or simple manual agriculture. Society provided all that was required without individual effort, leaving a centuries-long lifetime for the Eldar to spend satisfying their every desire. Fuelled by inexhaustible curiosity, many gave way to their darkest and most hedonistic impulses. Exotic cults sprang up all over the Eldar domains, each dedicated to esoteric knowledge or sensual excess.

As these cults gained a tighter hold over the Eldar, so their society became increasingly divided. Some heeded the portents that haunted their dreams, fleeing to found the Exodite colony worlds on the fringes of the Eldar empire. As their civilisation descended into anarchy, a few Eldar repented of their vices and fled into the void aboard space-borne craftworlds. Most glutted themselves on the pursuits of the depraved, and this corruption turned quickly to wanton abandon. In time, brother fought brother and sadistic killers stalked the shadows in search of victims for their vile lusts. No life was spared in the pursuit of pleasures both murderous and perverse. A sickness of vice overtook the Eldar race, and blood flowed through the streets amidst the bestial roar of the crowd.

> "What do Humans know of our pain? We have sung songs of lament since before your ancestors crawled on their bellies from the sea."
>
> **Farseer Eldrad Ulthran**

THE BIRTH OF A GOD

Only a fool would pretend to understand the strange otherworld that is the Warp, for it is, by its very nature, inconstant and incomprehensible. Yet it was within the Warp that the destruction of the Eldar race took shape. It was here amidst the swirling psychic energy that their corruption became manifest. Within the Warp, thoughts and emotions swell and grow, fed by fellow feelings until they achieve a consciousness of sorts. They become spirits of greater or lesser potency, and their long gestation is followed by birthing pains that rock the Warp and rupture the fabric of space. Amidst the swirling psychic energy of the Empyrean, the corruption of the decadent Eldar became manifest as their departing spirits began to coalesce into a gestalt consciousness.

What an unimaginably foul and sickening mind it was that the Eldar unknowingly raised in the Warp. It was a shadow of themselves, of what they had become, of nobility and pride brought low by perversity and shamelessness. For years the Eldar were riven with madness. Worlds burned as the Eldar slew and laughed and feasted upon the corpses of the dead, and slowly the Great Enemy stirred fitfully into life. Too late the Eldar realised that they had created a god in their own image, a god grown immense and potent by suckling upon the dark fodder of the Eldar spirit. No creature was ever conceived that was as terrible or perverse as the Chaos god Slaanesh, She Who Thirsts, the Doom of the Eldar incarnate.

When Slaanesh was finally born into divine consciousness there was not one Eldar alive who did not feel its claws in his soul. With a howl of raw power Slaanesh burst into supernatural life, and a psychic implosion tore at the universe. Billions upon billions of Eldar screamed aloud in agony and fell dead. In a heartbeat, the Eldar civilisation was snuffed out, leaving a pulsing afterbirth of pure chaos in its place. The spirits of the Eldar were drawn from their minds and consumed as their blasphemous creation took its first infernal breath. Intoxicated with this draught, Slaanesh laughed and looked upon a universe of gods.

THE DYING

The epicentre of the psychic apocalypse lay within the gilded heart of the Eldar realms. All Eldar within thousands of light years were reduced to lifeless husks, their spirits sucked into the Warp. Most of those who had foreseen the catastrophe and fled upon the craftworlds were overwhelmed, with only those furthest from the devastation surviving. The remote Exodite worlds remained largely untouched. Within the space of a single moment the Eldar had become a doomed people, knowing that their nemesis was born and would hunt them for the rest of eternity.

The psychic shock wave focused upon the Eldar, but millions of Humans, Orks and creatures from other races were destroyed too. Warp space convulsed as a cosmic hurricane raged across the galaxy. The fabric of reality was torn apart and the Warp spilled from the dimensional rift into the material universe, turning hope into despair and paradise into hell. Psykers of all races howled with pain as their people died in storms of blood and madness.

The rent in space roiled and spread until it completely encompassed the Eldar realms of old. Today this gaping lesion is known as the Eye of Terror, the largest area in the galaxy where the Warp and the material universe overlap. Daemons bathe in the energy of the

Warp, whilst Daemon Princes and the worshippers of Chaos rule over planets turned into nightmare worlds of fire and darkness.

Ten thousand years before the Fall, the Warp was riven with storm and tempest. This made it almost impossible for Human spacecraft to travel between the stars. With the birth of the Great Enemy the Warp was temporarily calmed, its rage all but spent. A new equilibrium was reached as Slaanesh joined the ranks of the Chaos gods. With the Warp storms around ancient Terra dispersed, Human worlds throughout the galaxy were brought into contact once more. During the Great Crusade that followed, the Emperor brought Humanity together and forged the Imperium of Man. In this way the death of the Eldar heralded the birth of the Imperium, and Mankind inherited the stars.

THE MYTHIC CYCLES OF THE ELDAR

The Eldar cling tenaciously to their ancient folklore. The characters and events of legend are commonly discussed and comparisons drawn between mythic events and those of the present day. Every Eldar is familiar with the epic songs and dances that form their mythic cycles, and references to these tales are immediately understood by other Eldar. It is as if the myths are bound within the Eldar psyche, and contemporary events and decisions are constantly reinterpreting the ancient tales.

The principal characters of the mythic cycles are the gods, their mortal descendants the Eldar, and the monstrous adversaries they fought. The chief and oldest of all the gods is Asuryan, the Phoenix King. His first brother is Kaela Mensha Khaine, which means bloody-handed Khaine. Khaine is the god of both war and murder, and he symbolises wanton destruction and martial prowess. Third of the greatest

gods is Vaul, the crippled smith god who is often depicted chained to his own anvil. Isha is the goddess of the harvest, and it is from Isha that the Eldar race is descended. The youngest goddess is Lileath the Maiden, who is mistress of dreams and fortune. The third of the trinity of Eldar goddesses is Morai-Heg the Crone, an ancient and withered creature who holds the fates of mortals inside a skin rune pouch.

As well as the many gods there are countless mortal heroes descended from the gods, who founded the great houses that are remembered even amongst the Eldar of the craftworlds. These include the great hero Eldanesh, who was slain by Khaine and whose blood is said to drip from his arms and hands. Eldanesh had many descendants, the Eldanar, of whom Inriam the Young was the last. Rivals to Eldanesh were the descendants of his brother Ulthanash, who in time became as great as the Eldanar.

THE MURDERED PANTHEON

The Eldar say that their gods are dead: Slaanesh destroyed them and stole their power. Nonetheless there remained some ideas and values that were lodged so firmly into the Eldar psyche not even ultimate degradation could erase them from the racial consciousness. This incorruptible spirit is represented by the most powerful of the ancient Eldar gods.

Two Eldar gods of old survived the Fall. The Laughing God Cegorach, worshipped by the enigmatic and lethal Harlequins, survived through guile alone. The other survived through might; he that is known as Kaela Mensha Khaine, the strongest and most warlike of all the Eldar deities.

Tradition has it that Slaanesh and the Bloody-handed God fought a titanic battle in the Warp. Despite Khaine's divine might and mastery of war, Slaanesh, glutted upon the power of the gods, eventually proved the stronger.

Exhausted from the struggle, the Great Enemy was not powerful enough to destroy the Eldar god completely. Instead Kaela Mensha Khaine was rent into many fragments and driven out of the Warp forever. Each fragment ultimately came to rest within the wraithbone core of a craftworld, where it took root and grew into an Avatar of the Bloody-handed God. These Avatars of Khaine lead the Eldar to war to the present day.

THE HARLEQUINS OF THE LAUGHING GOD

When an Eldar dies his spirit is caught within his crystal spirit stone and so escapes the Chaos god Slaanesh who would otherwise consume it. The craftworld Eldar release this spirit into the infinity circuit, and the spirits of the Exodites find similar refuge within the world spirit of their home planets.

The Harlequins, however, belong to the Laughing God. Their dying spirits merge together with their patron, strengthening his power. The only Harlequin

not protected in this way is the Solitaire, who plays the role of Slaanesh in ritual performances, and whose spirit already belongs to the Great Enemy.

The story goes that while Slaanesh fought with Kaela Mensha Khaine, the Laughing God escaped into the webway and hid amongst its myriad tunnels. He lives there still, laughing at the gods of Chaos, emerging randomly to play his deadly tricks upon them or make his secret plans. He cannot be caught, for he is too fast and subtle, and he knows all the secrets of the webway.

Of all the Eldar, the Harlequins of the Laughing God are the most mysterious, and many credit them with supernatural powers. No one knows where they come from. Some claim that they guard the secrets of the webway's endless paths and tunnels. Even to other Eldar they are other-worldly creatures, whose origins and fate seem curiously different from that of the rest of their race.

Harlequins have no home craftworld of their own. Instead, they travel the webway, moving between the Eldar craftworlds as if guided from place to place by some unknown purpose. In peacetime the Harlequins weave spells of song and dance, enacting the mythic cycles of the Eldar in mime and music. When war calls they lend their strength to the might of the Warrior Aspects and Guardians. The Harlequins always seem to appear upon the eve of momentous events, whether for good or ill, and their appearance is said to be a portent of the shifting tides of fate.

The strangest of all Harlequins is the Solitaire, who lives apart from all other Eldar. He speaks and is spoken to only in ritual form, and when he is not performing he rarely communicates with the other Eldar. It is said that to speak to the Solitaire or to cross his path is to invite damnation, and that if a person were to accidentally address or touch the Solitaire it would be better that he ended his life there and then rather than suffer the terrible doom that awaits him.

THE EXODITES

During the Fall the degeneration of the Eldar did not go wholly without resistance. Some, the more prescient, began to openly criticise the laxity of their fellow citizens, and to warn against the effect of pleasure cults. Soon the general collapse of society convinced even the most resolute amongst them that there would be no end to the reign of death and depravity. Some decided to leave the Eldar worlds, and settle new planets free of creeping corruption.

These Eldar are known as the Exodites. Of all the Eldar race they were uniquely far-sighted. Amongst a race naturally indulgent and hedonistic they were reviled as dour fanatics obsessed with misery and gloom. There were some whose dire premonitions were perhaps yet another form of insanity, simply one more conceit taken to inhuman extremes. Others were genuine survivalists who chose exile over degradation and destruction. In an assortment of spacecraft the Exodites abandoned their homes. Many died out in open space. Some reached new worlds only to be slain by marauding Orks or slavering predators. Many more survived. For the most part they headed eastwards as far away from the main concentration of Eldar worlds as they could reach.

Upon the fringes of the galaxy the Exodites made new homes. The worlds they settled were savage and life was often hard for a people unused to physical work and self-denial. When the final cataclysm erupted most of the Exodite worlds were far from the epicentre and survived. Many craftworlds rode out the psychic shock wave, but the Exodites had already reached places of safety – or else they perished with the rest of their race and have been forgotten.

The Exodite worlds are untamed and often dangerous planets. Most are home to large herds of megadons that the Exodites know by the name of dragons. It is likely that these creatures were once native to only one particular region, but the early settlers spread them throughout all their worlds so that they are now common. The Exodites follow the dragon herds as they graze the endless grasslands of the great plains. Although this lifestyle is in many respects a primitive one, the Exodites have many advanced technologies and are familiar with all the sophisticated materials used on the craftworlds. It is by choice that they live as they do, and their way of life has proven every bit as successful as that of the other Eldar.

> "The mind of the Farseer is utterly inhuman in its depth and complexity. Without mercy or moral feeling, his consciousness stands upon the edge of spiritual destruction. That he does not fall must be a result of constraints and balances that only an Eldar could understand. To a mere Human it is yet another reminder that we are but children in comparison to that ancient and powerful race."
>
> **Inquisitor Czevak**

THE DARK KIN

At the moment of Slaanesh's birth, the centre of the ancient Eldar empire was destroyed and the Eldar all but wiped out. It was believed by the craftworld Eldar that they and the Exodites were the only survivors. Centuries later, reports spread of ancient Eldar vessels plying the void once more; of depraved and vicious pirates intent on bloodthirsty raiding.

It is a great mystery how the Dark Eldar escaped the Fall even as it eradicated their civilisation, but like a canker in the hidden dimension of the webway they survive to this day. Preying upon all others, the Dark Eldar are a violent reminder of the depths to which Eldar society plummeted.

THE MAIDEN WORLDS

When their civilisation was all-powerful the Eldar settled many new worlds. They learned how to turn barren, lifeless places into planets suitable to live on. Hundreds of otherwise uninhabitable places blossomed into life and became paradises ripe for settlement. Most of these worlds were destroyed during the Fall, swallowed into the Eye of Terror. Their Eldar populations were eradicated by the psychic shock-wave of the Warp space rift and destroyed or else changed in ways too horrible to contemplate. When the Eldar worlds were destroyed there were many worlds on the distant fringes of Eldar space that had been seeded, but which were not yet ready to inhabit.

These worlds were not touched by the Fall, and continued to develop in the manner intended by the now dead Eldar. The Eldar of modern times refer to these now habitable planets as the Maiden worlds or Lileathan worlds after Lileath, the moon goddess of Eldar folklore. As far as the Eldar are concerned the Maiden worlds are Eldar planets, created by their forefathers for them to settle. Many of the Maiden worlds have since been discovered and settled by other races, especially by the Imperium. The Eldar regard this as nothing less than invasion, and the settlement of Maiden worlds is the most common cause of conflict between the Eldar and Mankind.

THE ELDAR PATH

The Eldar of the craftworlds have developed strict controls over their own inner natures so that their civilisation will never again fall to Slaanesh. Every Eldar chooses for himself a discipline that he then makes his task to master to the exclusion of all else. Each discipline is called a path, and each path may necessitate further choices and specialisations.

Once an Eldar has mastered one path he chooses another, and in this way builds up a repertoire of abilities over which he has complete control. An Eldar may travel many different paths in his life, and the skills he learns in each path serve to enrich further accomplishments. In this way the Eldar avoid temptation and tame their wanton natures. To the Eldar all paths are strewn with dangers, for the Eldar mind is capable of depth and understanding that goes beyond the concept of mere Human obsession. Such dangers are likened to traps or nets, waiting to catch the unwary upon the Eldar path and hold him fast forever. When an Eldar's mind becomes so tightly focused upon one thing that he can no longer make the change to another path then he is said to be lost upon the path. This is a terrible and frightening fate for all Eldar, as it is a fate that can befall any of them despite the discipline and training that they receive. In the case of the Warrior Path these individuals are called Exarchs, and there are other examples of this fate such as the Crystal Seers and the doomed Bards of Twilight.

There are innumerable paths, some as rare as the Path of the Seer, some as common as the Path of the Artisan. Each offers its followers a complete way of life. The Path of the Seer is the most treacherous and complex of all, but Eldar who have mastered the less esoteric paths are no less respected than their brethren. The artisans are the Eldar who create the craftworlds and their contents, calling masterpieces into being with the care a musician lavishes upon his harp or a warrior upon his sword. It is from the ranks of those upon 'civilian' paths such as these that the Eldar Guardians are mustered in times of need.

THE WAY OF WAR

The Eldar are a race beset on all sides by warfare. Would that it were not this way, for Eldar generations are few and far between and they can ill afford to lose their numbers. Young Eldar often believe they can rebuild their glorious empire with fire and passion, but the Seers know well that their shattered civilisation is locked in a struggle for simple survival.

When the Eldar go to war, they do so as a group of specialists that perfectly complement one another's role upon the battlefield. Each unit plays its own part with the skill of a virtuoso, their abilities combining in a symphony of destruction that is far greater than the sum of its parts. From the most numerous horde to the mightiest enemy war machine, there is an Eldar squad with skills and wargear perfectly suited to its annihilation. Combined with the prescience of the Farseers and the strategic genius of the Autarchs, even a small strike force can devastate its chosen opponents before they can muster an effective counter-attack. The Eldar ideal is to slaughter those who oppose them without a single loss from their own ranks; the usurpers are many and the Eldar are few. They cannot afford to throw away their lives in the manner of the soldiers of the crude races.

THE TEARS OF ISHA

One of the oldest and most important Eldar myths recalls how the Eldar race was born of Isha, the goddess of the harvest, and Kurnous, the god of the hunt. Lileath, Isha's daughter, dreamed that Khaine would be torn into a hundred pieces by a great mortal army. When Khaine learned of this, he flew into a tempestuous rage and resolved to destroy the Eldar race. He pursued them through the universe, trapping and slaying many before Asuryan heard the weeping of Isha and so learned of Khaine's plan. To save the few who remained, Asuryan placed a great barrier between mortals and gods, dividing them for all eternity.

This went very hard with Isha, who now wept all the more because her mortal children had been separated from her. Isha and Kurnous pleaded with Vaul the Smith to help them. Vaul knew that Asuryan would never change his mind, but his heart was softened by Isha's plea. From her tears Vaul made the spirit stones, by means of which Isha could see and talk to her children.

One day Khaine overheard Isha as she spoke to her children and he immediately told Asuryan. The Phoenix King was very angry that his commands had been disobeyed. He told Khaine that as Isha and Kurnous had betrayed him, Khaine could do with them as he wished. This suited Khaine very well, as he still feared that Lileath's prophecy would be fulfilled. He made the god and goddess his prisoners, and though he could not slay them he ensured that they endured constant torment and confinement.

THE PATH OF THE WARRIOR

The Path of the Warrior teaches the arts of death and destruction. Due to the dark side of the Eldar psyche, it calls to almost all Eldar at some point in their long lives. Exactly what draws an Eldar onto the Path of the Warrior is uncertain. Perhaps it is the recognition of an innate destructive impulse in the dark side of their psyche that only ritual training and combat can purge. In aeons past, the ancient Phoenix Lords taught the arts of war to both male and female Eldar, and as a result Eldar warriors are as likely to come from either sex.

As with many of the more complex paths, the Warrior Path is divided into many separate ways. Each of these is known as a Warrior Aspect, representing a different facet of the Eldar war god Khaine, and bringing with it unique fighting techniques, weapons and abilities.

The Aspects differ greatly in their methods of warfare, and offer many specialist skills designed for specific battlefield roles. Each Aspect upon a craftworld keeps at least one shrine in which to practice the mastery of their Warrior Path. When the Eldar go to war the Warrior Aspects fight in a predetermined role associated with their shrine. They have their own

warrior garb, a form of ritual battle suit, and distinctive weaponry. Their minds and bodies are honed with endless exercise, both physical and spiritual, until they become suffused with the Aspect of Kaela Mensha Khaine that their shrine represents. The Aspect Warriors do not live in the shrines, and when they put aside their ritual masks and uniforms they can walk at peace through their craftworld. Only the keepers of each shrine, the Exarchs, live within them.

Some Aspects are unique to specific craftworlds. Others are common to most, including the Dire Avengers, the Howling Banshees, Striking Scorpions, Fire Dragons, Swooping Hawks, and Dark Reapers.

> "The stars themselves once lived and died at our command, yet you still dare to oppose our will."
>
> **Farseer Mirehn Bielann**

EXARCHS

An Eldar who is lost upon the Path of the Warrior is called an Exarch. Such a fate does not befall an Aspect Warrior quickly, but the repeated exhilaration of battle can act like a dangerous drug upon a warrior's psyche. Aspect Warriors learn how to control their warrior-selves, putting on and casting aside their blood-hungry persona as they don or discard their ritual costumes. An Aspect Warrior who becomes an Exarch loses this ability to dissociate himself. This has serious consequences because an Exarch's only impulse is to wage war; all other feelings are subordinated to that single deadly desire.

The Exarchs are the high priests of Khaine the Bloody-handed God and keepers of the shrines of the Aspect Warriors. Exarchs do not leave their shrines except in times of war or high conclave. Even the smallest shrines are extensive structures with areas dedicated to training, instruction, and ceremony. Each shrine has its own armoury, and its own inner sanctum where the Exarchs administer the rites of war before the altar of the Bloody-handed God. It is here that the Exarchs recite the battle songs of old and mark the warriors' bodies with runes of blood before they don their armoured suits in readiness for war. In this way the Exarchs are the priests and guardians of the shrines, as well as armourers and instructors who will guide their fellow Eldar along the Path of the Warrior.

An Exarch wears an elaborate and often ancient version of the ritual Aspect Warrior armour. He boosts his already superhuman abilities with arcane wargear, and wears upon his suit the spirit stones that contain the departed spirits of all the suit's past Exarchs. Each Exarch assumes the sacred name associated with this suit, and his spirit mingles with those of all the Eldar who have borne it since the shrine's inception. Thus an Aspect Warrior who becomes an Exarch is reborn as an ancient warrior hero. Memories and experiences of departed Exarchs merge with the new bearer, and the heroic ideal of that Aspect is reborn in new flesh. Invariably their weapons are extremely potent and their abilities are far more developed than even the finely honed warrior skills of the Aspects. It is the presence of the spirit-pool of raw psychic energy that gives the suit and warrior (for the two are indistinguishable) their special warrior powers.

OUTCASTS

Sometimes the rigid constraints of the Eldar path are intolerable even for an Eldar to bear; such individuals leave their craftworlds and become Outcasts. Many Eldar spend years or decades as Outcasts before they return to the Eldar path. Outcasts must bear the terrible burden of their heightened Eldar consciousness without the protection of the Eldar path. Set free within the universe they are dangerously vulnerable. Their psychically sensitive minds are a beacon to predatory daemons and in particular to the Great Enemy Slaanesh. Only Eldar of especially strong character can survive for long as Outcasts. After years of adventure and wandering, or sailing the seas of space aboard the pirate fleets, most Eldar eventually return to the sanctuary of the Eldar path.

There are many kinds and degrees of Outcast. They leave their craftworlds and live elsewhere, often wandering the galaxy and visiting the worlds of Men or the Exodites. They are welcome aboard craftworlds only briefly, for their minds are dangerously unbounded and attract predators from the psychic realms of the Warp. Daemons or other Warp entities can home in to the mind of an Outcast and lodge in the psycho-supportive environment of the craftworld's wraithbone core. Outcasts are also disruptive in another sense, for their presence can distract the young and inexperienced from the Eldar path by their romantic tales of travel and freedom.

Some Eldar yearn for the undiscovered vistas of open space. They join fleets of exploration and disappear into the untrammelled warp space tunnels of the webway. Most do not return, though a few come home laden with alien treasures. They bring tales of new worlds, fabulous discoveries, and courageous battles on the edges of the galaxy. It is not unknown for Humans to come into contact with these adventurers, for these are the only Eldar a Human is likely to meet other than on a battlefield.

The wildest of all the spacefaring Eldar become corsairs and raiders. They often continue to trade and visit their craftworld or the Exodite worlds whilst plundering the ships of Humans, Orks and even other Eldar. They even sometimes hire out their services to alien races, while many voyages of exploration soon turn into military ventures. As home and the Eldar path become increasingly remote, the naturally wild and amoral character of the Eldar resurfaces. Eldar pirates are quick tempered and unpredictable, equally inclined to magnanimity and wanton slaughter. Fleets such as the Eldritch Raiders, the Steeleye Reavers and the Sunblitz Brotherhood are greatly feared by the star systems they regularly plunder.

To the ignorant, there is little to distinguish between the ships of the craftworlds, the Corsair fleets of Outcasts and the Dark Eldar pirates. All are seen as a constant, elusive menace that bring sudden death to the unwary. On occasion, Corsair fleets will join with the ships of a craftworld in response to a common threat, while at other times a craftworld may aid its Corsair cousins on a mission of war against alien vessels, all of which adds to the illusion that the Eldar as a whole are little more than a race of piratical raiders.

The wanderlust that lurks in the heart of every Eldar can be expressed in many forms. Some Eldar leave for the distant Exodite worlds, living for many years amongst the Exodites, though they are rarely ever truly accepted by their new hosts. Other Outcasts become Rangers, and travel from world to world to experience the glories and perils of the galaxy. These Rangers send news to the craftworlds whilst adventuring for ancient treasures and spiritual enlightenment. Many Eldar simply lose themselves in the webway, occasionally to be found by the Harlequins or drifting towards the nightmare city of Commorragh. Whatever their exploits when they are away, if an Eldar returns to the craftworld and steps upon the path again, all earlier misdeeds are forgotten as they take up their disciplined life once more.

THE SWORDS OF VAUL

Isha and Kurnous suffered the fiery torments of Khaine's confinement for countless years. Bound with bonds of flame and scorching iron, the god and goddess were cast into a burning pit out of the sight of mortals and gods. Of all the gods only Vaul the Smith pleaded for them, and eventually he swore an oath to Khaine that he would make a hundred swords in exchange for their release, for Vaul was the greatest swordsmith of all eternity and a single blade forged by his hand was of incalculable value. A date was fixed one year hence for the completion of the bargain. When the time came for Vaul to deliver the weapons, he had still one unfinished blade. To conceal the shortfall, Vaul took an ordinary mortal blade and mixed it amongst his own work. At first Khaine was so pleased with the weapons that he failed to spot the deception. Only when Isha, Kurnous and Vaul were far away did he discover the forgery. He roared with anger, calling Vaul a cheat and crying out for vengeance. This was the beginning of the long struggle between Khaine and Vaul, which is called the War in Heaven.

THE ELDAR CRAFTWORLDS

Before the Fall, the space-cities that were the called the craftworlds fled from the encroaching cataclysm, carrying a tiny proportion of the Eldar race to safety and permanent exile. Some craftworlds survived for hundreds, or even thousands of years before their people faded and died, while others endure to this day. Many floated into the void and were lost forever in regions of space that remain dark and unexplored. They may be there still, lonely and forgotten voices in the wilderness of deep space.

Each craftworld originated from one or more of the ancient Eldar planets. Over the centuries the craftworlds' occupants sought out other surviving Eldar amongst the far-flung Exodite colonies, and even began to settle new worlds of their own. In this way the paths of Eldar and Mankind met for the first time and Humans became acquainted with the most ancient and enigmatic of the galaxy's living races. The names of the greatest craftworlds were soon heard upon Human lips: Alaitoc, Iyanden, Biel-Tan, Saim-Hann and Ulthwé. Yet to this day it is doubtful that more than a few Humans have ever set foot upon an Eldar craftworld.

IXIA WAYPORT, BIEL-TAN CRAFTWORLD

1 Naiad class cruiser	**4** Tower of Voidsight
2 Dome of Tears	**5** Spiritspire D'harquese
3 The Everguard	**6** Bridge of Transient Sighs

THE WEBWAY

The Eldar craftworlds float in deep space and move at only sub-light speeds. Their exact locations are not known by other races, and the Eldar themselves do not consider their physical positions to be important – rather nothing more than a momentary detail in an eternal journey. Smaller Eldar spacecraft, moored in docks upon the craftworld's fringes, travel between the different craftworlds by means of the webway. The main gateways into the webway take the form of swirling spheres of light and darkness held in stasis astern of each craftworld.

The webway is a labyrinth that exists between the material dimension and the Warp, part of both and yet not wholly in either. Created by technologies once taught to the Eldar by the ancient races known as the Old Ones, its pathways lead to the craftworlds, to the surface of the verdant worlds of the Exodites and to untold thousands of other worlds throughout the galaxy. Though the webway still connects many Eldar planets and craftworlds to one another, the baleful energies of the Fall have ruptured its hyperspatial pathways in countless places. Amongst the webway's shattered and treacherous tendrils there are many byways, dead ends, and mazes that can entrap the unwary. Some lead to places long since abandoned or destroyed, or else inhabited by the daemons of the Warp. These doors are sealed with runes of power, lest unknown horrors gain access to the craftworld or

THE BLACK LIBRARY

The Black Library is spoken of as a craftworld, which in form it may be, yet it is very different from the other craftworlds of the Eldar. Where the craftworlds float through the firmament of the material universe, the Black Library exists only within the webway itself. To reach the Black Library it is necessary to travel the secret passages through the warp, to pass its terrifying sentinels, and to find one of the hidden entrances that lead within.

The Black Library houses all the Eldar's most precious knowledge, and in particular all that they have learned about the perils of Chaos. It was Chaos that destroyed their once great civilisation, and which threatens them still from the Warp. The secrets of the library are not for the unwary or the merely curious. Within its psychically locked rooms lie grimoires of dark magic, black tomes of daemonic lore, and records of countless Chaos Cults throughout the galaxy.

Of all Humans, only a handful of Inquisitors of the Ordo Malleus have ever entered the confines of the Black Library, and then only in the company of Harlequins and under the closest supervision. None have ever described their experiences. These Inquisitors share a common bond with the Harlequins, for both are sworn enemies of Chaos and understand only too well the nature of the threat that faces Eldar and Humanity. As to the sentinels of the Black Library, their true nature remains an unspoken secret, yet they are described as the most terrible of all perils in the webway and the most dreaded individuals amongst all of the Eldar kindreds.

some unwary traveller unwittingly open a doorway and be sucked into warp space. The craftworld Seers claim there are many secret paths that lead through time and reality, though only the elegant and deadly Harlequins are reputed to know of such routes. Mighty Dark Eldar cities and nests of wasp-like Psychneuein infest its furthest reaches, but the best hidden of all the realms in the webway is the Black Library.

The exact shape and form of the webway is not fully understood by the Eldar of the present day. Knowledge of the myriad secret ways is considered of such importance that the Eldar no longer share its secrets with humans. Each craftworld's place in the webway is known only to its Seers. It is rumoured that a map was made many thousands of years ago, which is now kept in the Black Library. Although it is no longer entirely accurate, it shows many secret ways that have since been lost or forgotten. If this is so then the Guardians of the Black Library have chosen to keep their secrets, and one can only imagine that they have good reason to do so.

It is with this network that the Eldar ply the galaxy and wage war. The arterial passageways are large enough to carry spacecraft, though most tunnels only allow strike forces of Eldar on foot or small vehicles to pass.

Eldar spacecraft can travel through the Warp itself, although this is a slow and dangerous process for them. As a result the Eldar travel infrequently to places that lie more than a few light years from their webway portals. Webway journeys are relatively fast, enabling space fleets to move easily between the network's major gateways. This enables the Eldar to move swiftly to places directly connected by the labyrinth dimension, but makes it extremely difficult for them to reach worlds that have no gate into the network.

ELDAR TECHNOLOGY

The basis of Eldar technology is psychic, and is unique to the Eldar. No other race has ever replicated their technology, nor have the Eldar adopted much from the 'primitive' races that have inherited the galaxy. The brutality and ignorance of Mankind appals the Eldar, whilst the aloof arrogance of the Eldar race has never fostered the trust of the adepts of the Imperium.

Eldar technology adheres closely to natural biological shapes and structures. This is quite understandable, as there is no real difference between technology and nature in the Eldar mind – they are a single process by which the Eldar imbue living things with function and functional things with life. The materials the Eldar use in their engineering are complex and varied psychoplastics that can be readily formed into solid shapes under psychic pressure. In some respects they are more like living tissue than inert substances, growing and reacting to their environment in a similar way to plants. The completed device is a semi-organic machine or component that works in a conventional manner, though it is often operated by psychic means.

The most unusual of these psycho-plastics is called wraithbone: an immensely resilient substance, more difficult to damage than adamantium, and far more flexible. If it is damaged it will gradually repair itself, and the process can be accelerated by the psychic abilities of a Bonesinger. The only artefacts more precious to the Eldar than those made of wraithbone are the Tears of Isha, also known as spirit stones.

"A craftworld is sentient being, with a hundred thousand minds."

Inquisitor Czevak, the Living Worlds

A LIVING WORLD

All the craftworlds are built upon a skeleton of wraithbone whose structure extends throughout the gigantic craft. A similar wraithbone core lies at the heart of most large devices and every Eldar spacecraft. In function these cores are similar to the blood vessels and nervous system of a living creature, pumping life-giving energy around the body and also transmitting the impulses that coordinate its many functions. Wraithbone is psycho-conductive, and the core of a craftworld acts as a self-replenishing reservoir of power. The invasive rib-like structures carry this energy throughout the entire length and breadth of the craft.

In a very real sense, the craftworld is a living entity, powered by psychic energy and responding in an organic way to the stimuli of psychic forces. The power contained within it can be expended as light and heat, and most ship-board devices could not actually function without the psychic power grid that runs throughout the substructure of the craftworld. The Eldar refer to this grid as the infinity circuit.

SPIRIT STONES

Every Eldar wears a shining gem or polished stone upon his breast. This psycho-receptive crystal is called a waystone, and is attuned solely to the mind of its owner. Its purpose is to capture the psychic energy of the Eldar when it is released at the moment of death, becoming a spirit stone. As such energies carry with them a large part of an Eldar's sense of identity, personality, and memories, it is quite correct to think of this psychic energy as a soul.

If an Eldar's spirit is not captured by his waystone it is sucked into the nightmarish depths of the Warp. To a Human, such a fate means nothing, for virtually no Human mind is strong enough to retain a sense of consciousness after death – the psychic energy of the Human mind being paltry compared to that of an Eldar. Yet for an Eldar to enter the Realm of Chaos as a conscious spirit represents the ultimate horror. In the Warp there is nowhere an Eldar spirit can hide from the predations of Slaanesh; the nemesis of the Eldar awaits to consume them as it did their ancestors. To perish in this way is the ultimate fear for the Eldar. It is little wonder that the Eldar prize their spirit stones more than life itself, and will go to incredible lengths to preserve and recover them.

THE INFINITY CIRCUIT

When an Eldar dies his spirit stone is retrieved and implanted inside one of the craftworld's bio-domes. Here the wraithbone core lies exposed underfoot, and the spirit stones placed there quickly take root. The spirit is released into the infinity circuit, where it joins the eternal shades of the craftworld's dead. It says much about the Eldar's attitude to death that they choose the endless twilight of the infinity circuit over the alternative. Like spirit stones, the infinity circuit is one of the most precious resources of a craftworld and Eldar do not speak of its existence to other races.

Once he is part of the circuit an Eldar continues to exist forever, safe from the predations of the Warp, though his individual consciousness remains as a potential within the circuit. The infinity circuit is therefore far more than a source of energy, it is a place of refuge and eternal rest, from where the dead continue to watch over the living. Such is the plight of the Eldar that the living are sometimes forced to call their ancestors from their rest, transferring them into wraith-constructs so that they may fight for their craftworlds once more.

WORLD SPIRITS OF THE EXODITES

Every Exodite world has its own equivalent to the infinity circuit called the world spirit. Exodites too wear spirit stones and when they die they are taken beneath the earth into one of the great tribal barrows. They are laid to rest there and their spirit stones are broken upon the altars of the world spirit. Each world spirit is a complex psychic energy grid that extends over the entire planet, stretching between the tribal barrows,

CRAFTWORLD KEY

- ✝ ALAITOC
- ⚕ ALTANSAR
- ⚜ BIEL-TAN
- 🗡 IL-KAITHE
- 森 IYANDEN
- 🌿 IYBRAESIL
- 🌼 KAELOR
- 🍃 LUGGANATH
- 🜊 SAIM-HANN
- 🦅 ULTHWÉ
- 🕯 YME-LOC

stone circles and standing stones. These important places are where the spirit world and the material world can interact, where the spirits of the dead can flow together, and where the living can talk to the dead if they have the power.

The stone circles and standing stones are made from psychically interactive crystal. These towering stones are gigantic spirit stones that anchor psychic power into the earth. The links between them form part of the Eldar webway, but the paths from the webway into the world spirits are well hidden and protected. The most potent link in the entire world spirit network is the royal circle of the planet's king. This impressive structure consists of a system of concentric circles connected by avenues of megalithic spirit stones. The royal circle is supported by outlying menhirs that carry power throughout the entire planet and focus the energy of the world upon that one spot.

ELDAR LANGUAGE

It is almost impossible for an outsider to understand anything but the most basic attributes of the Eldar language, as many of its references draw directly upon the Eldar psyche, mythical peoples and places, and long-lost times and events. The Eldar also communicate with pose and gesture; it is possible for two Eldar to have an entire conversation with body language alone.

The Eldar written language is similarly complex. Each symbol, be it script, rune or hierogram, is not a simple letter form like the written Gothic of the Imperium but a symbol of a concept. Even more strangely, many of these word-concepts have a subtly different meaning when committed to script, another when employed in the runecasting of the Farseers, and yet another when incorporated into the hierograms of the Eldar houses and design schools.

BIEL-TAN
THE SWORDWIND

> "We bring only death, and leave only carrion.
> It is a message even a Human can understand."
>
> **Reqhiel of the Sons of Fuegan**

Of all the craftworlds it is the Eldar of Biel-Tan who strive hardest to return the Eldar empire to its former glory. Consumed with bitterness, they wage a constant campaign of xenocide against those foolish enough to cross their path.

The militant Eldar of Biel-Tan place greater importance upon the Path of the Warrior than other craftworlds. They know that if a new empire is to be forged, it will be done in the crucible of battle, tempered in strife and quenched in blood. As a result, the Exarchs of Biel-Tan number more than any other craftworld. The deadliest of the Exarchs band together into a military force known as the Court of the Young King. The duties of this elite cadre include awakening the Avatar when mustering for war. Led by the embodiment of Khaine, the Aspect Warriors of Biel-Tan fight as if possessed, their barely harnessed rage driving them to acts of bloody slaughter.

The assembled warhost of Biel-Tan is known as the Bahzhakhain, meaning the Swordwind – also 'Tempest of Blades' or 'Frozen Leaves Falling to Cut' depending upon inflection. The Swordwind strikes swiftly and surely, relying on a focused assault that uses surprise and the immense fighting skills of its numerous Aspect Warriors to annihilate the enemy in one clean blow. Their foes will often be overrun before they even have a chance to realise their doom.

As the Eldar of Biel-Tan see it, when the time comes for the Eldar to reclaim what is rightfully theirs, the paradise planets of the Exodites will be the first staging points for their conquest. Due to this, the Biel-Tan Eldar see any colonisation by other races as a threat to the future growth of the Eldar empire. The incautious Explorators of the Imperium have often made planetfall on an Exodite world, only for their successors to find nothing but corpses that have been hacked to pieces and subsequently picked clean by indigenous predators.

The barbaric Orks in particular are hated by the Biel-Tan Eldar, as they can spread across a newly colonised world as rapidly as a plague. There have been many accounts throughout Imperial history of the Biel-Tan Eldar arriving to help a beleaguered Imperial garrison fighting against the Orks, only for the Aspect Warriors to turn on their erstwhile allies once the Orks have been destroyed. This percieved treachery is one of the reasons the Eldar are seen as fickle and untrustworthy by other races. The warriors of Biel-Tan care not, for to them all other races are usurpers to be culled without mercy.

THE REBORN
The rune the Biel-Tan use stands for the principle of reincarnation, a fate thought to have been reserved for every Eldar before the Fall. The name of the craftworld means 'Rebirth of Ancient Days'. For them, winter has fallen on the Eldar, but they are convinced that spring will soon return.

SAIM-HANN
THE WILD HOST

"The wind whipping across your face as your blades whip across the throats of the foe. It makes the blood sing."

Hrythar Dreamweave, Wild Rider

Saim-Hann was reputedly one of the first craftworlds to abandon the Eldar homeworlds as the Fall approached, and it is their culture that is closest to that of the Exodite worlds on the fringes of the galaxy. The practices of the Saim-Hann craftworld are seen as barbarous by the other craftworlds, for the Eldar of Saim-Hann are fierce warriors who place a higher value upon honour than their sophisticated kin. Their bravery is legendary, but their pride has frequently led them to fight unnecessary wars and even to initiate conflict with other craftworlds.

The most famous warriors of the Saim-Hann craftworld are the Wild Riders, warriors who speed into battle riding jetbikes and who excel at swift raids. These warrior kindreds have much influence on the craftworld. Nearly all Saim-Hann warriors, including the Seers, belong to one of the Wild Rider clans. Each of these clans is led into battle by a Wild Rider chieftain. The chieftain's closest family form the kinsmen, who paint their faces with hot blood on the eve of conflict and ride to war together. In much the same way, each unit of jetbikes or Vyper pilots is comprised of blood relatives, and tend to sport a banner showing their clan's rune. It is only during a Wild Rider's time as an Aspect Warrior that his familial ties are put aside, as devotion to the shrine overrules all other considerations.

The Saim-Hann Eldar observe many rites of passage, usually upon the verdant worlds of the Exodites. A common rite involves catching a daggersnake in mid-strike, as the serpent is the symbol of Saim-Hann. The jetbike-riding kindreds excel at mimicking the strike of a snake upon the field of battle, and all Saim-Hann warriors have a tattoo of a serpent somewhere upon them. Saim-Hann is the craftworld with the largest proportion of Shining Spears Aspect Warriors, dauntless lancers who ride at the head of the Wild Rider strike forces.

The warriors of Saim-Hann always honour their debts. They are quick to swear blood bonds and are even rumoured to drink from each other's wrists during these ceremonies. However, the culture of Saim-Hann often leads to internal strife. Unlike other craftworlds, who unite in mass mobilisation, the Saim-Hann kindreds are free to choose whether to uphold a particular cause. This sometimes leads to Wild Rider families fighting amongst themselves, though these battles generally take a ritualistic form, consisting of single combat between champions. First blood is sufficient, but the frequently fatal consequences of these duels account for the reputation of the Wild Riders of Saim-Hann as feral savages amongst other Eldar.

THE COSMIC SERPENT

This is the symbol of the Saim-Hann craftworld. In Eldar myth, the Serpent is the only creature believed to exist in both the material and the psychic universes at the same time. Hence, the Serpent is said to know all secrets past and present. Saim-Hann means 'Quest for Enlightenment', for the Eldar word for snake and secret knowledge is identical: 'Saim'.

ULTHWÉ
THE DAMNED

"He who sees his own doom can better avoid its path.
He who sees the doom of others can deliver it."

Eldrad Ulthran, Farseer of Ulthwé

Craftworld Ulthwé is home to the most powerful psykers in the galaxy. The Eldar of Ulthwé have cast themselves as sentinels, keeping an endless vigil over the Eye of Terror. They maintain that their elite cadres of Farseers and Warlocks are needed to keep watch for the many and varied guises of Chaos. Other craftworlds whisper that Ulthwé has damned itself – that the Eye of Terror that has tainted the inhabitants of Ulthwé and exaggerated their psychic potential.

Ulthwé's many talented psykers can foresee future events with a greater precision than those of other craftworlds. This foresight allows them both to preserve their line and thwart their eternal enemies, the forces of Chaos. Of all the craftworlds, it is Ulthwé that intervenes most in the affairs of other races to further their own agenda.

Once led by the legendary Farseer Eldrad Ulthran, the Seer Council of Ulthwé has constantly influenced the course of history. At the behest of the Council, the craftworld's warriors are frequently sent into apparently unrelated battles that will ultimately concern Ulthwé itself. It is largely from these seemingly arbitrary conflicts that the Eldar have earned their reputation for random and capricious behaviour. But the Farseers of Ulthwé know well that stopping the fall of a single stone can sometimes prevent an avalanche, and they will often manipulate the Imperium in their quest to divert history. After all, the Seers of Ulthwé would rather see a hundred thousand Humans perish than a single Eldar life slip away.

Though the battle-psykers of Ulthwé have made their armies mighty indeed, continued reliance upon them has left the craftworld lacking in Aspect Warriors. The Path of the Seer is the longest and most treacherous, leaving little time for an Eldar to focus upon the Path of the Warrior. It is for this reason that, unlike its sister craftworlds, Ulthwé maintains a large standing army of Guardians.

During the Chaos Lord Abaddon's 13th Black Crusade, the Guardian-heavy armies of Ulthwé were organised into small but deadly strike forces that erupted from the webway in a string of lightning attacks. Led by the mighty Phoenix Lord Maugan Ra and guided by the masterful Eldrad Ulthran, these strike forces stole victory from Chaos forces upon dozens of battlefronts. More than ever before, the Black Guardians of Ulthwé are known and feared throughout the region around the Eye of Terror, both as saviours and dreaded foes.

THE EYE OF ISHA
This rune depicts the sorrow of Isha, the fertility goddess from whom the Eldar say they descend. It is the symbol of Ulthwé, whose name is a contraction of 'Ulthanash Shelwe' meaning the Song of Ulthanash. This ancient lay describes the feuding between the houses of Ulthanash and his brother Eldanesh.

ALAITOC
THE STARSTRIDERS

> "There is no corner of the galaxy
> that has not felt the eagle-keen gaze of Alaitoc."
>
> **Elarique Swiftblade, Autarch of Alaitoc**

The Eldar of Alaitoc are puritanical adherents to the Path of the Eldar, and they shun contact with outside influences. This zealous and restrictive attitude has led to many of Alaitoc's Eldar sating their repressed wanderlust by becoming Outcasts – either banished to the stars by their masters for some slight misdeed, or tiring of the harsh discipline of their craftworld. These nomadic individuals often undertake dangerous quests on behalf of their kin, and have become synonymous with Alaitoc across the breadth of the galaxy.

Although disenchanted with the strictures of their home, those that become Outcasts remain loyal to Alaitoc. Some become Corsairs, bolstering Alaitoc's formidable navy in times of war, their brightly-coloured starships in stark contrast to the midnight hulls of the main fleet. Others choose the way of the Ranger, acting as the craftworld's eyes and ears on the field of battle.

The nomadic Rangers of Alaitoc have a loose alliance with the Harlequins, regularly sharing knowledge about the furthest corners of the webway. These two factions also complement each other's skills on the battlefield. When the Alaitoc fight a war, they gather many Rangers, sending them ahead of their main force to sow disruption and anarchy in the enemy army. The Rangers are highly skilled at remaining unseen whilst pinning down enemy units and breaking apart any cohesiveness their armies might have. When the rest of the Alaitoc force closes in, the enemy army is depleted and confused – easy prey for the Aspect Warriors and Harlequins closing upon their positions.

Some Rangers ultimately become Pathfinders, losing themselves as Outcasts in the same way an Exarch dedicates himself to the Path of the Warrior. These individuals are supernaturally adept at concealing themselves and killing from afar. Some amongst these near-invisible assassins revere the mysterious wanderer known as Hoec, he who is said to be one with the webway, and who has walked the paths between planets since the stars themselves were young.

It is through the Rangers of Alaitoc, or Starstriders as they call themselves, that the Imperium has gleaned much of its knowledge about the Eldar. This is not a gift Alaitoc has willingly given, but a product of excruciation at the hands of the Imperial Inquisition. It is this fact that led to the ongoing Beelze conflict, and the current state of war that exists between the Imperium and Alaitoc – a war that Imperial commanders have often compared to hunting ghosts.

THE DOOM OF ELDANESH

Eldanesh was an Eldar hero who was slain by the jealous war god Khaine. The symbol of Alaitoc depicts the sword of Khaine bisecting the Red Moon, the sign of Eldanesh. The Red Moon is an ill omen for most Eldar and the Alaitoc use it to remind themselves of what happens if mortals offend the gods.

IYANDEN
THE GHOST WARRIORS

"The dead must join our ranks,
lest we be forced to join theirs."

Prince Yriel, Autarch of Iyanden

Once the largest and most populous of the craftworlds, Iyanden has been reduced to a shadow of its former glory in a bitter war with the Tyranid race. It was an attack by the Tyranid hive fleet known as Kraken that rang the death knell for the craftworld. Iyanden was too slow to outrun the Tyranid invasion and was all but destroyed. Thousands upon thousands of its warriors fell in battle against the Great Devourer. On the verge of utter defeat, Iyanden was saved from extermination by the return of Prince Yriel and his Eldritch Raiders. The Corsair captain engaged the hive fleet in space, destroying its grotesque mother ships before taking the fight to the enemy upon the surface of Iyanden. Despite eventual victory, the craftworld is unlikely to ever recover its losses and many of its Seers believe the Eldar of Iyanden are on the brink of extinction.

The profound loss suffered by Iyanden has led to a continuing reliance upon the wraith-constructs that now form the backbone of the craftworld's armies. Silent squads of Wraithguard and magnificent Wraithlords tower above Iyanden's remaining Guardians and Aspect Warriors, wielding the most powerful weaponry the craftworld can provide. But such strength comes at a great price, for the wraith-constructs of Iyanden are inhabited by the departed spirits of Iyanden's dead.

Were it not for the direst necessity, the Seers of Iyanden would leave their ancestors to rest. However, the fight for the survival of their craftworld forces them to resurrect their dead and enlist them to fight once again. This process is akin to necromancy in the Eldar mind. The soul must be summoned from the infinity circuit into a psycho-crystalline spirit stone and subsequently interred in the impregnable wraithbone shell of a construct. Even the lowliest Wraithguard can take incredible punishment and survive, but on the rare occasions that one is destroyed, its spirit stone will be recovered and rehoused in another shell. In this way the dead of Iyanden are trapped in an eternal cycle of war.

The psykers that specialise in summoning ancient heroes and guiding them on the field of battle are known as Spiritseers. The greatest of the craftworld's Spiritseers is Iyanna Arienal, the Angel of Iyanden, who is accompanied in battle by a giant wraith-construct animated by the spirit-pool of a mighty Exarch. Like all her kin upon Iyanden, she is determined that the flame of her craftworld will blaze brightly once more rather than flicker and die out.

THE SHRINE OF ASURYAN
Asuryan is the oldest and greatest of the ancient Eldar deities. He is the father of the gods, the ancestor of all living things. This is the symbol of the Iyanden craftworld whose name means 'Light in the Darkness', a reference to the ever-burning shrine of Asuryan, the flame of hope for the Eldar of Iyanden.

FORCES OF THE ELDAR

This section of the book details the forces at the craftworlds' disposal – their weapons, the units, and the historical 'special characters' that you can choose, such as Prince Yriel of Iyanden and the mighty Phoenix Lords. Each entry describes the unit and gives the rules to use them in your games of Warhammer 40,000. The rules are broken up into categories:

Special rules: These are rules that make each unit exceptional. These always apply to that unit.

Wargear: Almost all Eldar units have ritual wargear mentioned in their description. Some is automatically included with that unit, whereas other items of wargear are optional – this is detailed in the army list. In the case of Aspect Warriors, Exarch wargear items are also listed. Only Exarchs may take these ancient and powerful artefacts.

Exarch Powers: Aspect Warrior entries also include details of supernatural abilities available to their Exarchs at the points cost in the army list.

Note that Exarch powers can only ever affect Aspect Warriors and Autarchs in the same squad as the Exarch using them. If an Exarch is removed from play then his abilities are lost.

Surrounded by glittering statues of pure crystal, a Farseer stands deep in
concentration. Around him orbit glowing runes in the same the way as planets orbit a sun, but this solar
system describes not space, but time. The Farseer raises a delicate hand and plucks a burning rune from its
erratic orbit before it touches any of the others.
He frowns at it for a long second, and bows his head.

In the cool depths of the craftworld, a Spiritseer glides through the mists of the Chamber of Fallen Heroes.
Ranged along the vaulted walls are green-lit alcoves containing statuesque wraith-constructs. As he reaches
each alcove, the Spiritseer pulls a glittering gemstone from his robe and, with great care, transfers one into
each warrior shell in turn. One by one, the statues start to come alive.

A circle of female Aspect Warriors stands in an arena of slender white pillars.
Their strident voices keen through the air as they sing the Hymn of Khaine. They move in a synchronised
dance, activating the plates and clasps of their bone-white Aspect armour one by one in a ritual pattern.
Finally, the warriors don their maned helmets, completing
the transformation into faceless, emotionless killers.

The Young King fixes his gaze on the opposite wall as his attendant Exarchs move
around him silently. They are painting blood runes of war on his naked body. The blood dries instantly, and
it burns corrosively into his skin like a net of fire. The fate that awaits him behind the bronze doors of the
Avatar's chamber is polarised into a single point of time.
It bears down upon him like a ball of fire.

The swirling wraithgate in the midst of the mustered warhost crackles and spits. As one
the chanting Aspect Warriors around it fall to one knee. A moment passes, then suddenly the Avatar of
Khaine bursts from the portal in a storm of flame. The sand vitrifies in the towering warrior's footsteps. He
stalks toward the lip of the ridge. He looks down with contempt on the enemy armies.
The Avatar raises his weapon to the skies and emits an ear-splitting roar.
The Eldar raise their voices as one, and fall upon the prey below.

Blood Runs. Anger Rises. Death Wakes. War Calls!

ELDAR WEAPONRY

So advanced is Eldar technology that to the lesser races such weapons are things of witchcraft, capable of breaking the laws of nature and tearing holes in the fabric of reality. To the Eldar, each weapon is a thing of macabre beauty, perfectly suited to the art of death.

THE STORM OF BLADES

The Eldar are famed for their widespread use of shuriken weaponry. A shuriken weapon is designed to generate a hail of razor-sharp monomolecular discs.

Ranging in size from sidearms to tank-mounted cannon, all shuriken weapons work on the same principle. The ammunition is stored as a solid core of plasti-crystal material. A series of high-energy impulses originate at the rear of the weapon and fly through the barrel at terrific speed. Each impulse detaches a monomolecular slice of the ammunition core and catapults it from the weapon's barrel, allowing the weapon to fire up to a hundred bladed discs in a burst of a few seconds.

THE WEAVER OF RUIN

The Eldar make use of monofilament weapons, all of which work in a similar fashion by creating a dense monofilament mesh from a complex organo-polymer compound. This is released through thousands of microscopic firing ducts and woven into a net of monofilament wire by spinning gravity clamps. The victim's own struggles bring about his doom, for the razored net is so sharp it can reduce an entangled enemy into bloody chunks of flesh in seconds.

THE DELIVERER OF FATE

Unlike the simple rocket-firing tubes employed by the Imperium, Eldar missile launchers use complex chambered pods that contain several different kinds of ammunition, all but eliminating the need to reload.

THE FURY OF THE STARS

The Adepts of the Imperium have attempted to harness plasma technology, but only the Eldar have truly mastered its potential. To the Eldar it is further testament to the idiocy of Man that he has created a weapon that frequently maims or even kills the wielder. The starcannons of the Eldar have no such flaws. Each weapon's plasma core produces the incandescent heat of a sun, but sophisticated containment fields ensure that the weapon remains cool to the touch.

THE SPEAR OF LIGHT

Eldar laser weapons use psychically grown crystals to filter and refine laser bursts to their optimum potency. Many Eldar consider the laser weapon the most elegant of all, exulting in the fact that their technological mastery extends even to light itself.

THE SUNDERED VEIL

The most dangerous of all the Eldar guns are those that enable their user to open a portal to the hellish dimension of the warp. Both the D-cannon and the wraithcannon use warp technology to collapse an area of the material universe, effectively piercing a hole in reality. If the target is not wholly swept into the Immaterium, it is usually torn to pieces by the violent and extreme forces brought to bear upon it.

THE TOUCH OF DEATH

The weapons wielded by the Eldar in close quarters combat are just as deadly as their guns. The gently purring motors of their chainswords spin glittering monomolecular-edged teeth. Shimmering fields dance along the keen edges of their swords, glaives and knives, and plasma grenades blossom into white-hot death as the Eldar close in for the kill.

WEAPON	RANGE	STRENGTH	AP	TYPE
Bright lance	36"	8	2	Heavy 1, Lance
Eldar missile launcher (krak)	48"	8	3	Heavy 1
Eldar missile launcher (plasma)	48"	4	4	Heavy 1, Blast, Pinning
Flamer	Template	4	5	Assault 1
Scatter laser	36"	6	6	Heavy 4
Shuriken cannon	24"	6	5	Assault 3
Shuriken catapult	12"	4	5	Assault 2
Shuriken pistol	12"	4	5	Pistol
Starcannon	36"	6	2	Heavy 2

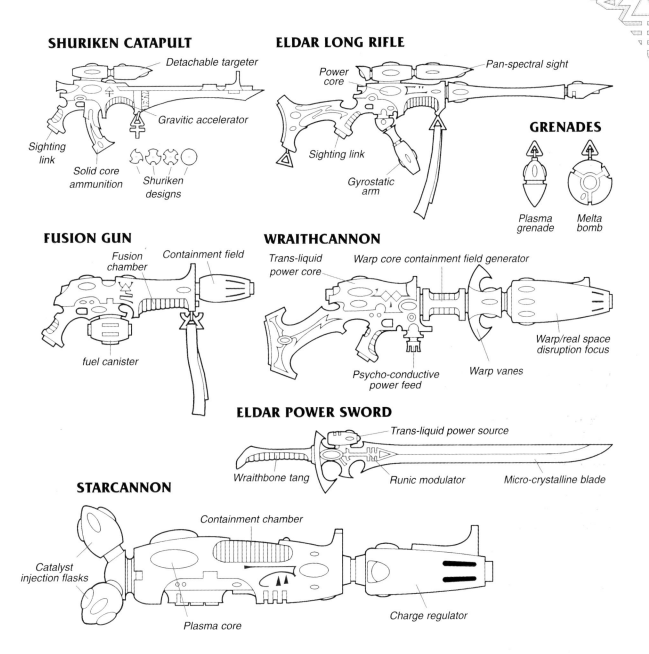

SHURIKEN CATAPULT

Detachable targeter

Gravitic accelerator

Sighting link

Solid core ammunition

Shuriken designs

ELDAR LONG RIFLE

Power core

Pan-spectral sight

Sighting link

Gyrostatic arm

GRENADES

Plasma grenade

Melta bomb

FUSION GUN

Fusion chamber

Containment field

fuel canister

WRAITHCANNON

Trans-liquid power core

Warp core containment field generator

Psycho-conductive power feed

Warp vanes

Warp/real space disruption focus

ELDAR POWER SWORD

Trans-liquid power source

Wraithbone tang

Runic modulator

Micro-crystalline blade

STARCANNON

Containment chamber

Catalyst injection flasks

Plasma core

Charge regulator

ELDAR ARMOUR

In place of thick armour plates used by the foot soldiers of the Imperium, the Eldar use psychically activated bodysuits. Guardians wear armour formed from complex psycho-plastics which stiffens with the impact of a shot or blow. Aspect Warrior armour is similar in design but incorporates moulded plates to better reinforce the suit. Both are constructed of a psycho-sensitive material that reacts to the movements and thoughtforms of the wearer, moulding and reshaping itself to fit like a glove as the warrior moves and fights. Even the heaviest and most ornate of these suits, worn by the Exarchs, are still lightweight compared to the bulky armour of other races.

The Eldar also use force fields varying from personal shield projectors to the holo-fields employed by grav-tanks and their gigantic titans. Some are stranger in function still. These include the psychic shielding of rune armour, said to pulse in time with the wearer's heartbeat, and the arcane holo-suits used by the Harlequins, which project dazzling domino fields.

THE AVATAR
OF THE BLOODY-HANDED GOD

Deep in the heart of every craftworld lies a single sealed wraithbone chamber. Inside, upon a smouldering throne, sits an Avatar of the Bloody-handed God – a terrifying statue of immobile iron. His slitted eyes reveal an empty darkness as if his whole body were a hollow metal shell.

As the craftworld prepares for war the psychically receptive chamber pulses with the battle-lust of the Eldar. In response, the Avatar begins to glow as the heat of his fiery blood is kindled. Molten iron boils through his veins, so that he crackles and hisses like a furnace.

Through the naked ribs of wraithbone a psychic roar echoes throughout the craftworld. Summoned by this battlecry, the Exarchs bring the Young King, an Aspect Warrior chosen by the Farseers. He stands naked in front of the door of the chamber, painted head to toe with the blood-runes of Kaela Mensha Khaine and crowned with a garland of thorns.

As the ceremony grows more intense so the Bloody-handed God stirs into life. Every single Eldar feels the Avatar's inhuman blood-thirst awakening in his own mind until, at last, the bronze doors of the Avatar's throne room swing open. The light that spills out is so bright that it burns through eyelids into the mind, and the sound of splintering iron is deafening. Into the throne room the Young King walks, every step taking him nearer fiery destruction as the bronze doors close behind him.

For several hours the furnace rumbles and booms, mercifully drowning out the screams of the Young King. At last there is an inhuman roar of agony and a psychic shock wave blows apart the gates of the shrine. Amidst the blistering torrent the smouldering Avatar stalks from his throne room into the craftworld.

The living Avatar is an ancient god incarnate. Molten iron flows through his veins and bubbles of fiery ichor burst and solidify upon his skin. Tendrils of smoke and flying cinders enwreathe him like a dark crown, and thick red gore oozes from his hands and drips from his fingers. In his right hand he carries the Wailing Doom, the weapon of the Bloody-handed God that shrieks as it tastes mortal flesh. The runes upon its blade writhe as they struggle to escape their bondage, as if tortured by the Avatar's fiery grasp.

As to the fate of the Young King, not even the Farseers will speak. Perhaps he lives on for all eternity, his spirit intermingling with the greater spirit of Khaine. More likely he is incinerated utterly, his spirit a sacrifice to the merciless Bloody-handed God.

THE AVATAR OF KHAINE

	WS	BS	S	T	W	I	A	Ld	Sv
Avatar	10	5	6	6	4	6	4	10	3+

SPECIAL RULES

Daemon: To all intents and purposes, an Avatar is a Daemon and will therefore be affected by weapons and abilities that affect Daemons. He benefits from a 4+ invulnerable save as well as his 3+ armour save.

Fearless: The Avatar is the living incarnation of a god and is hence Fearless.

Inspiring: When led by their Avatar, the craftworld Eldar are filled with thoughts of bloodshed, and its presence inspires them to great acts of valour. Any Eldar unit with a model within 12" of the Avatar becomes Fearless.

Molten Body: The Avatar's body is fashioned from burning iron flooded with glowing magma. Melta weapons, flamers and heavy flamers cannot wound the Avatar.

Monstrous Creature: The Avatar is a huge and fearsomely strong opponent and is therefore a monstrous creature.

WARGEAR

The Wailing Doom: The Wailing Doom is a weapon of immense power that may take the form of a vicious spear, a mighty sword or a many-bladed axe. It can be used to project a nimbus of burning psychic energy, using the following profile:

Range: 12"   S:8   AP:1   Assault 1, Melta

"Perfidious Eldar! These aliens had the stars in their grasp and now are left to sift the dust of their once fabulous realm. For all their intellect and mysticism they could not contain the beast within them, nor tame the wild monsters of the Shadow. Why should we pay them any heed?"

- **Gründwald, Ordo Xenos**

FARSEER

The Path of the Seer is the most dangerous and convoluted path of all, for psykers are intimately connected with Warp space. To proceed too quickly along the Witch Path would be to invite the most heinous damnation, as the minions of the Great Enemy lurk within the Warp ready to rend the souls of overambitious Seers. Furthermore, the Witch Path itself can entrap an adherent for the rest of his life. Just as Eldar who are trapped on the Warrior Path become Exarchs, so Seers who progress too far along the Witch Path become Farseers.

Farseers are masters of prediction, and are the eldest and most experienced of a craftworld's advisors. Even in battle they can perform their divinations, casting the complex wraithbone runes of the Eldar and interpreting changes in the glowing icons as they orbit around them. In this way the Farseers explore the myriad skeins of past and future, studying the manifold consequences of the smallest decision the better to guide their people to victory.

Just as the Farseers guide the fate of the craftworlds, so they guide their armies in times of war. A Farseer can uncover the enemy's intentions, calculate the likely effects of his clumsy attacks, and guide him to his doom. The Farseer himself fights with a grace that makes the enemy seem predictable and slow, flowing around blasts of fire without breaking stride. So powerful is a Farseer that he can obliterate an enemy leader's mind or hurl a battle tank into the air. In the crucible of battle, Farseers shape the future with the skill of master craftsmen – their tools are the warriors they lead, and their clay the flesh of those who oppose them.

	WS	BS	S	T	W	I	A	Ld	Sv
Farseer	5	5	3	3	3	5	1	10	–

SPECIAL RULES
Fleet of Foot, Independent Character.

Psychic Powers: A Farseer is a psyker and must choose between 1 and 4 Farseer psychic powers. A Farseer can use a single psychic power per turn.

WARGEAR
Rune Armour: All Farseers wear a wraithbone breastplate shaped into runic forms that ward off enemy attacks. A model wearing rune armour has a 4+ invulnerable save.

Ghosthelm: A Farseer's ghosthelm incorporates intricate crystalline psychic circuitry that masks their spirit in the Warp. If a Farseer suffers a Perils of the Warp attack his ghosthelm will prevent it on a D6 roll of 3+.

Runes of Warding: A Farseer can use runes of warding to throw up psychic interference to hinder his foe. All enemy Psychic tests must be taken on 3D6, suffering a Perils of the Warp attack on any roll of 12 or above.

Runes of Witnessing: A Farseer uses runes of witnessing to guide his second sight along the twisting strands of fate. A Farseer with runes of witnessing rolls 3D6 and discards the highest roll when taking a Psychic test. You must use the lowest two rolls.

Spirit Stones: A Farseer can use the power of a spirit stone to charge themselves with psychic energy. A Farseer with spirit stones can use two psychic powers per turn. A Farseer cannot use the same psychic power twice in the same turn.

WARLOCKS

The most aggressive and warlike of all the Witch Paths is that of the Warlock. Warlocks are Seers who once trod the Path of the Warrior, and it is their previous experience as warriors that enables them to harness their destructive impulses in battle. The ornate helmets worn by Warlocks are kept in the shrines of the Warrior Aspects. A Warlock can only become his warrior-seer self by returning to a shrine and receiving his helmet from an Exarch as part of the blood-ritual of the Aspect Warrior.

A Warlock not only learns the runes of war but also how to wield the witchblade, a powerful Eldar force weapon. Witchblades writhe and twist with living runes, and focus the power of the Warlock's mind into destructive energy through a helical psychic matrix running through the blade. In the hands of a Warlock, a witchblade strikes with a devastating burst of force that can incinerate a foe where he stands.

When the Eldar go to war their Warlocks accompany them. They use their psychic powers both to protect the Eldar warriors and to bring havoc to their enemies; a thought-wave from a Warlock can instil courage in his cohorts or sear the souls of his foes. Though not as powerful as Farseers, few psykers of other races can equal the arcane might of an Eldar Warlock or match them in battle.

	WS	BS	S	T	W	I	A	Ld	Sv
Warlock	4	4	3	3	1	4	1	8	–

SPECIAL RULES
Fleet of Foot.

Warlock Powers: Each Warlock is a psyker and may be given a single Warlock power at the points cost listed in the army list.

Spiritseers: Those rare Warlocks who specialise in summoning and guiding the spirits of the dead are called Spiritseers. Any Wraithlord or Wraithguard unit with a model within 12" of a Spiritseer need not test for Wraithsight.

WARGEAR
Rune Armour: All Warlocks wear a wraithbone breastplate shaped into runic forms that ward off enemy attacks. A model wearing rune armour has a 4+ invulnerable save.

Witchblade: Warlocks wield witchblades, see the Warhammer 40,000 rulebook.

Singing Spear: The singing spear is a psychically-charged weapon similar to the witchblade, but it can also be thrown at opponents (it returns automatically to the user's hand). The spear can be used in close combat, but it requires two hands and so the wielder cannot gain the extra attack from an extra hand weapon. Like witchblades, singing spears wound on a 2+, but when rolling to damage a vehicle they have a Strength of 9. When thrown, singing spears have the following profile:

   Range: 12"   S: X   AP: 6   Assault 1

FARSEER PSYCHIC POWERS

Unless otherwise noted, these powers work as described in the Psychic Powers section of the Warhammer 40,000 rulebook, are used at the start of the Eldar turn and do not require the Eldar psyker to have line of sight to target.

Doom: The Farseer searches for the thread of destiny that spells the destruction of an enemy and draws it into being. The Farseer can target any non-vehicle unit within 24". All hits caused upon that unit gain a re-roll to wound until the start of the next Eldar turn.

Eldritch Storm: The Farseer summons a corona of crackling energy that strikes out with arcs of lightning and hurls enemies in all directions. This psychic power is used in the shooting phase instead of firing a weapon. The Eldar player places the large blast marker centred on an enemy model within 18". Vehicles touched by the template suffer a hit with 2D6+3 armour penetration and are spun around to face in a direction determined by the scatter dice – if a hit is rolled the Eldar player may choose its facing.

> Range: 18" S: 3 AP – Pinning, Large Blast

Fortune: The Farseer scries the strands of the future to foresee where the enemy will attack, warning his fellow Eldar so that they may avoid enemy fire. Nominate one Eldar unit with a model within 6" of the Farseer. This unit re-rolls any failed saves it makes until the start of the next Eldar turn.

Guide: The Farseer's prophetic powers warn him of the enemy's foul intent, allowing him to direct the fire of his warriors. Nominate one Eldar unit with a model within 6" of the Farseer. This unit re-rolls any failed to hit rolls made in that turn's shooting phase. If the unit is using a guess range weapon (such as a D-cannon) you may re-roll their scatter dice instead.

Mind War: The Farseer reaches out to destroy the mind of an enemy with an irresistible mental onslaught. This psychic power is used in the shooting phase instead of firing a weapon. The Eldar player may choose any unengaged model within 18" of the Farseer and within his line of sight (models mounted in vehicles cannot be targeted). Both players roll a D6 and add the Leadership of their respective models. For each point the Farseer wins by, the target loses a wound, with no armour saves allowed.

WARLOCK POWERS

A Warlock's power is available permanently, so he does not need to take a Psychic test to use it.

Conceal: The Warlock clouds the minds of the enemy, creating a shifting psychic mist that conceals his unit. The Warlock's whole squad receives a 5+ cover save. This does not count as occupying cover for the purposes of assault.

Destructor: The Warlock focuses his anger and hatred and unleashes it at the enemy in a roiling blast of raw psychic power. Destructor is used in the shooting phase instead of firing a weapon. It is worked out like a normal shooting attack with the following profile:

> Range: Template S: 5 AP: 4 Assault 1

Embolden: The Warlock instils an unshakeable courage in his comrades, reaching into their minds with visions of mighty heroes and great victories. The Warlock and his squad may re-roll any failed Leadership tests.

Enhance: The Warlock empowers his fellow warriors with lightning speed and skill. All models in the same unit as the Warlock, including the Warlock itself, add +1 to their Weapon Skill and Initiative. The effects of multiple Enhance powers are not cumulative.

AUTARCH

Autarchs are the supreme commanders of the Eldar warhost, and have a consummate understanding of the art of war. Held in high esteem by seer and soldier alike, each Autarch has mastered many paths over the centuries, including one or more of the facets of the Warrior path. At some point in their lives all Autarchs start developing a passion for command and strategy.

Autarchs believe the true path to martial excellence lies not so much in the heat of mêlée, but rather in gaining a wider vision of the battle and directing the Eldar warhost on the most lethal and efficient way to victory. This is the Path of Command, a burning obsession with truly understanding how each mission can be made part of a complex battle plan, and in turn each battle can be made part of a grand war plan. To guide them along this path, Autarchs draw their inspiration from the mythical leaders of the great Houses of old, such as Eldanesh, Ulthanash and Bierellian.

An Autarch's insight into the specialities of each element of the Eldar way of war gives him an unparalleled strategic ability that an Exarch, obsessed with one facet of war, could never hope to achieve. When an Eldar army is led by an Autarch it functions as a well-honed machine, each component acting in perfect concert with the others. However, it is not purely as a commander that the Autarch excels. When the battle-lust calls, he will spearhead assaults, duelling with the leaders of the enemy armies or destroying war machines with contemptuous ease. Winged Autarchs will often soar at the head of their forces, swooping down into the fray to change the course of a conflict with a single well-placed kill.

	WS	BS	S	T	W	I	A	Ld	Sv
Autarch	6	6	3	3	3	6	3	10	3+

SPECIAL RULES
Fleet of Foot, Independent Character.

Master Strategist: Autarchs are superb strategists, able to command the Eldar units in perfect synchronicity. Any Eldar army including one or more Autarchs has a strategy rating of 4. While the Autarch is alive, you may choose to add 1 to your rolls for reserves, regardless of whether he is in play or not (a roll of 1 always counts as a failure).

WARGEAR
Forceshield: The Eldar favour sleeve-mounted field projectors over the clunky and restrictive armour used by other races. A forceshield confers a 4+ invulnerable save.

"Only when you have soared through the morning skies on wings of flame can you understand the Hawk. Only when you have fallen screaming upon those who know they are already dead can you understand the Banshee. Only when you have annihilated those who would oppose you can you truly understand the power of the Dragon. And only one who has travelled but ultimately turned away from each of these paths can understand the Autarch."

**Anthrillien Morningchild,
Autarch of Yme-Loc**

DIRE AVENGERS

The Dire Avengers are first amongst the Aspect Warriors of the Eldar. They represent the War God as noble warrior, and are merciless to their foes and unstinting in their devotion to their people.

Most common of all the Aspect Warriors, the Dire Avengers can trace their line back to Asurmen, first of the Phoenix Lords. They are famed for being as deadly on the attack as they are stalwart in defence, and are widely regarded as the most tactically flexible of all the aspects. A famous Eldar legend tells of a single squad of Dire Avengers holding a nightmarish tide of daemons at bay to allow their comrades to escape. Such acts of valour are commonly echoed by their modern counterparts.

Dire Avengers are armed with shuriken catapults – a weapon perfected by the Eldar and especially deadly in the hands of these Aspect Warriors. They consider the wielding of the shuriken an art form, and even carry these lethal discs under their robes when outside the shrine. In this way even an apparently unarmed Dire Avenger can slay an opponent with a swift gesture.

When in battle, Dire Avengers use their shuriken catapults to create an impenetrable storm of monomolecular blades. They have an uncanny knack of knowing when to follow this onslaught with a lightning-fast assault and when to carefully draw the enemy forward onto their blades. It is rare to find an Eldar force without a squad of these graceful warriors at its heart.

	WS	BS	S	T	W	I	A	Ld	Sv
Dire Avenger	4	4	3	3	1	5	1	9	4+
Exarch	5	5	3	3	1	6	2	9	3+

SPECIAL RULES
Fleet of Foot.

WARGEAR
Avenger Shuriken Catapults: Dire Avengers use modified shuriken catapults with extended barrels, power feeds and inbuilt rangefinders. They have the following profile:

Range: 18" S: 4 AP: 5 Assault 2

EXARCH WARGEAR
Diresword: These weapons incorporate a spirit stone in the hilt that can sear the mind of the target. A diresword is a power weapon. In addition, if a model suffers any unsaved wounds from a diresword, it must immediately pass a Leadership test for each wound suffered. If any of these tests are failed, the victim dies automatically and is removed regardless of remaining wounds.

Shimmershield: A shimmershield is an advanced field projector that protects the user and his squad. A model with a shimmershield, and all members of his unit, will benefit from a 5+ invulnerable save in close combat.

EXARCH POWERS
Bladestorm: The Dire Avengers empty their weapons in a devastating hurricane of bladed discs. The Exarch and his squad may choose to add one to the number of shots they each fire with their shuriken weapons that turn. If they do so they may not fire in the subsequent shooting phase as they reload.

Defend: The Exarch leads his squad in a complex pattern of parries and dodges designed to avoid enemy blows. Enemy models directing their attacks towards the Exarch's squad lose one Attack in each assault phase (to a minimum of 1).

HOWLING BANSHEES

The banshee is a harbinger of woe and death in Eldar mythology, whose cry is said to herald ill fate and can even wrench a soul from its spirit stone. It is fitting that the most feared of all the Aspect Warriors draw their inspiration from this unearthly creature.

In Eldar myth, the Crone Goddess Morai-Heg sought to partake of the wisdom contained in her divine blood. Knowing there was only one with the power to harm a god, she sent her daughters to haunt their father Khaine's steps with their piercing screams. Promising an end to this curse, she bade Khaine cut off her hand that she might drink deep of her vitae. With this deed Morai-Heg gained the knowledge of blood, and the aspect of the banshee was granted to Khaine in return.

Howling Banshees are swift and athletic troops who are most deadly in hand-to-hand fighting. Their Banshee masks contain psychosonic amplifiers that magnify their keening battle screams into mind-destroying shockwaves. This inflicts severe damage to the central nervous system of the Eldar's foe, inspiring a feeling of mortal terror and causing momentary paralysis. A full squad of Banshees activating their masks in unison can cripple an enemy unit before a single blow is struck.

In battle, what these fierce warrior women lack in brute strength they make up for in precision and efficiency, their shimmering power swords slicing through armour, flesh and bone with equal ease.

	WS	BS	S	T	W	I	A	Ld	Sv
Howling Banshee	4	4	3	3	1	5	1	9	4+
Exarch	5	5	3	3	1	6	2	9	3+

SPECIAL RULES
Fleet of Foot.

WARGEAR
Banshee Mask: In the first round of an assault a model wearing a Banshee mask has Initiative 10 and negates any Initiative bonus conferred by cover and grenades.

EXARCH WARGEAR
Executioner: The executioner is a powered glaive capable of slicing an opponent in half with a single blow. It is a two-handed power weapon that adds +2 S.

Mirrorswords: Some Banshee Exarchs have mastered a deadly ambidextrous sword-form that uses paired blades. A model with mirrorswords counts as having an extra hand weapon that grants +2 A instead of the usual +1 A. Mirrorswords ignore armour saves.

Triskele: A triskele can be thrown in a great coruscating arc that slices through anything in its path. It can be used as a power weapon. It can also be used as a ranged weapon with the following profile:

Range: 12"   S: 3   AP: 2   Assault 3

EXARCH POWERS
War Shout: The Exarch uses her Banshee mask to unleash a terrifying howl of fury and despair. In the first round of an assault, any enemy unit she or her squad is fighting must pass a Morale test or count as having WS1 for the rest of that assault phase.

Acrobatic: The Exarch and her squad leap and bound forward when engaged in assault. They have the Counter-Attack special rule.

FIRE DRAGONS

The Fire Dragon aspect is modelled upon the dragon of Eldar myth, the sinuous fire-breathing reptile that represents wanton destruction. Fire Dragons are aggressive and warlike, and seek nothing less than the total annihilation of their chosen foes. They have an unsurpassed mastery of heat weapons, and take savage delight in the devastation they create. It is said their Exarchs generate a corona of lambent flame around themselves when the battle lust is upon them.

The role of the Fire Dragon is to attack enemy strongholds and war machines, using their deadly weapons to destroy well-armoured troops or emplaced weapons. They carry powerful fusion guns that can reduce an enemy to a cloud of superheated vapour in a second. Though short-ranged, these weapons are capable of turning even the heaviest battle tanks into piles of molten slag.

Should the Fire Dragons need to assault their target to ensure its destruction, they use discus-shaped melta-bombs that can be attached to any surface and detonated with a word. Nowhere is safe from the white-hot rage of the Fire Dragon, for even the mightiest fortification affords scant protection.

	WS	BS	S	T	W	I	A	Ld	Sv
Fire Dragon	4	4	3	3	1	5	1	9	4+
Exarch	5	5	3	3	1	6	2	9	3+

SPECIAL RULES
Fleet of Foot.

WARGEAR
Fusion Gun: The fusion gun has the following profile:

Range: 12"   S: 8   AP: 1   Assault 1, Melta

EXARCH WARGEAR
Firepike: The firepike is a sophisticated melta weapon, with a distinctive long barrel that can project its deadly melta beam a considerable distance.

Range: 18"   S: 8   AP: 1   Assault 1, Melta

Dragon's Breath Flamer: The dragon's breath flamer can unleash a raging inferno upon a nearby foe. It has the following profile:

Range: Template   S: 5   AP: 4   Assault 1

EXARCH POWERS
Tank Hunters: The Exarch has versed his squad well in the art of stalking armoured vehicles, able to spot weak points in the armour with uncanny speed. The Exarch and his squad have the Tank Hunter ability.

Crack Shot: The Exarch can pinpoint his targets with unerring accuracy. The enemy may not make cover saves against shots from the Exarch, and the Exarch may re-roll any failed to wound rolls when shooting.

"We warned you of the price of your actions, now you must pay it in full – in blood."

Message received prior to the Assyri Devastation

STRIKING SCORPIONS

The Warrior Aspect of the Striking Scorpion epitomises the deadly attributes of their namesake, and they are the most potent of all the close assault aspects. They are merciless killers without exception, revelling in the hunt and the kill. Perhaps the most sinister aspect of the Striking Scorpion is the legacy of their former master Arhra – the ability to stalk the shadows, creeping ever closer to their prey before falling upon them like the wrath of Khaine himself.

The heavier armour plates forming the Striking Scorpion's armour mean that they are not as swift as their Banshee sisters. Instead, these Aspect Warriors excel at stalking through dense terrain, using every available hiding place to close with their prey. When they launch their attack they use shuriken pistols and scorpion chainswords; vicious blades with diamond-toothed edges that mangle and tear flesh.

The signature attack of the Striking Scorpion is made by the weapon pods housed on either side of the warrior's helmet, known as mandiblasters. These are short-ranged laser weapons used to deliver a deadly energy sting in close combat. Activated by a psychic pick-up, they fire a hail of needle-thin shards that act as a conductor for a highly charged laser. A mandiblaster volley and the blistering storm of attacks from the Scorpions that follow it is enough to tear the heart out of an enemy force.

	WS	BS	S	T	W	I	A	Ld	Sv
Striking Scorpion	4	4	3	3	1	5	1	9	3+
Exarch	5	5	3	3	1	6	2	9	3+

WARGEAR

Mandiblasters: A model with mandiblasters has +1 A.

Scorpion Chainsword: This is a one-handed weapon that adds +1 S to the model's attacks.

EXARCH WARGEAR

Scorpion's Claw: The scorpion's claw takes the form of a powered claw-shaped gauntlet incorporated with a shuriken catapult. The claw may be used both as a power fist and a shuriken catapult in the same turn.

Chainsabres: Some Exarchs train in the use of blades paired with ancient gauntlets that house twin-linked shuriken pistols, allowing them to level a storm of attacks at their foes. A model with chainsabres has +1 Attack and can re-roll all failed to hit and to wound rolls.

Biting Blade: The teeth of a biting blade tear through flesh as if it were parchment, shredding muscle and bone. It is a two-handed close combat weapon that adds +1S. Furthermore, each hit scored by a model with a biting blade adds a further +1S for the purposes of resolving those attacks. For instance, an Exarch who hits three times will strike at S7.

EXARCH POWERS

Shadowstrike: The Exarch becomes one with the shadows, using them to shield his squad from their enemies as they approach. A squad including a model with Shadowstrike has the Infiltrate special rule. This ability cannot affect an Autarch – his command is needed elsewhere.

Stalker: The Exarch and his squad can flow silently and without trace through dense terrain. They have the Move Through Cover special rule.

DARK REAPERS

The Dark Reapers are the most menacing of the Warrior Aspects. They exemplify the War God as Destroyer, and their skull-masked costume echoes that of their founder, the Harvester of Souls. Their armour is the colour of midnight, and incorporates a complex set of interlocking plates. Although the Dark Reapers are comparatively slow as a result, this is of little consequence, for their role on the battlefield is long-ranged fire support.

The father of the Dark Reapers, Maugan Ra, teaches that the kiss of death can be delivered from afar. It is this credo that is central to the way of the Reaper. Their sacred weapon is the reaper launcher, a long-barrelled missile weapon that can create a blistering firestorm with a single salvo. The armour-piercing missiles it fires are powerful enough to take down all but the most heavily protected foe.

The Dark Reapers pride themselves on their accuracy. Their skills are increased still further by powered limb supports that absorb the recoil of the Reaper launcher, advanced sensor vanes upon their helmets that can lock onto a fast-moving target, and mind-links that allow a Reaper to 'see' from the muzzle of his weapon. Their superb aim enables them to dominate the battlefield, pinning down enemy forces and destroying their chosen targets at will.

	WS	BS	S	T	W	I	A	Ld	Sv
Dark Reaper	4	4	3	3	1	5	1	9	3+
Exarch	5	5	3	3	1	6	2	9	3+

WARGEAR

Reaper Launcher: The reaper missile launcher has the following profile:

Range: 48"   S: 5   AP: 3   Heavy 2

EXARCH WARGEAR

Tempest Launcher: The Exarch has an ancient reaper launcher that fires clusters of small reaper missiles in a great arc. It has the following profile:

Range: G36"   S: 4   AP: 3   Heavy 2, Blast

EXARCH POWERS

Fast Shot: The Exarch is adept at laying down a lethal hail of fire from any weapon, firing shot after shot into the enemy. He may add +1 to the number of shots fired by his weapon (so, for example, Heavy 2 becomes Heavy 3). Fast Shot may not be used by an Exarch in the same turn as he uses Crack Shot.

Crack Shot: The Exarch is a supreme master of all ranged weapons, able to pinpoint his targets with unerring accuracy. The enemy may not make cover saves against shots from the Exarch, and the Exarch may re-roll any failed to wound rolls when shooting.

SWOOPING HAWKS

The Swooping Hawks take their name from the wild hunting birds of the Eldar myths, synonymous with vengeance and retribution. In ancient times the Eldar believed that the spirit of a murdered Eldar would pass into a hawk and hover above the killer as a mark of guilt. The winged Aspect Warriors who take that hawk as their symbol, however, play a much more active role in their foe's destruction. The Swooping Hawks have the ability to launch high into the air at a moment's notice. Their wings are made from vibrating feather plates and incorporate small gravitic lifters. When the Hawks fly these wings vibrate with such speed they turn into a blur of colour. The ritual weapons of this Aspect are the lasblaster – a far more efficient energy weapon than the clumsy lasgun of the Imperium – and the grenade pack. Grenade packs contain both anti-personnel grenades for fly-by attacks and haywire grenades for disabling enemy artillery.

	WS	BS	S	T	W	I	A	Ld	Sv
Swooping Hawk	4	4	3	3	1	5	1	9	4+
Exarch	5	5	3	3	1	6	2	9	3+

SPECIAL RULES
Fleet of Foot.

WARGEAR
Lasblaster: The lasblaster has the following profile:

Range: 24"   S: 3   AP: 5   Assault 2

Swooping Hawk Wings: A model with Swooping Hawk wings moves as if equipped with a jump pack and may use the Deep Strike rules to deploy in missions that allow it.

Swooping Hawk Grenade Pack: Any time a Swooping Hawk unit uses its Deep Strike ability, it may place a single large blast marker centred on an enemy model anywhere on the table and roll a scatter dice. If an arrow is rolled, the marker scatters D6" in the indicated direction. Work out hits and damage as normal.

Range: n/a   S: 4   AP: 5   Large Blast

Haywire Grenades: The Eldar use haywire grenades for disabling enemy vehicles. They send out a powerful, short-range electromagnetic pulse that shorts out electrical wiring and disrupts the energy systems of its target. A model attacking with these grenades may only make a single attack. If it hits, roll a D6 to determine the effect:

1 = no effect, 2-5 = glancing hit, 6 = penetrating hit.

EXARCH WARGEAR
Hawk's Talon: A swooping Hawk Exarch often carries a much more powerful version of the lasblasters wielded by his squad. It has the following profile:

Range: 24"   S: 5   AP: 5   Assault 3

Sunrifle: The sunrifle is an energy weapon potent enough to slay whole squads with a burst of dazzling laser beams. It has the following profile:

Range: 24"   S: 3   AP: 5   Assault 6, Pinning

EXARCH POWERS
Skyleap: With a great shout, the Exarch and his squad launch high into the sky. The player may elect to remove a unit with Skyleap from the table in its movement phase, placing it in reserve. If the squad was engaged in combat, the enemy may make a 3" consolidation move. The squad may then Deep Strike back into play from their following turn, exactly as if they had been held in reserve from the beginning of the game (even in missions that do not allow Deep Strike or reserves). For example, if they are removed from the table on turn 2, they will re-enter play on turn 3 on the roll of a 3+.

Intercept: The Exarch and his squad are so skilled at aerial combat that they can disable even speeding enemy skimmers. In assaults, they never require worse than 4+ to hit a vehicle.

WARP SPIDERS

The Warp Spiders take their name from the tiny but aggressive creatures that are seen amongst the slender wraithbone trees of the Dome of the Crystal Seers. These sparkling entities can move anywhere within the craftworld, melting their arachnoid bodies into the infinity circuit and crystallising to reappear at a new location. They are attracted in vast numbers to invasive psychic entities, which they hunt and destroy much like an immune system.

The Warp Spider Aspect Warriors epitomise this doctrine of aggressive defence. Using a compact warp-generator housed within their armoured backpack, they can to make short warp-jumps, disappearing and reappearing in the blink of an eye.

This enables them to make totally unexpected attacks on their foes, though it does necessitate spending a short time in the Warp. For this reason the Warp Spiders are considered the bravest of all Aspects – they risk not only their lives in the name of victory, but also their souls.

The ritual armament of the Warp Spider is the death spinner; a highly advanced weapon that extrudes a thick cloud of razor-sharp monofilament wire. The spinner's magnetic containment field then spools the wire together and hurls it toward the enemy. The wire's own tension causes it to writhe and lash, and where it touches flesh or soft tissue it slices through the victim's body, causing an agonising and messy death.

	WS	BS	S	T	W	I	A	Ld	Sv
Warp Spider	4	4	3	3	1	5	1	9	3+
Exarch	5	5	3	3	1	6	2	9	3+

WARGEAR

Death Spinner: This weapon has the following profile:

Range: 12"   S: 6   AP: –   Assault 2

Warp Jump Generator: A unit with warp jump generators moves as if it was equipped with jump packs. If unengaged, the unit may make a second jump during the assault phase instead of assaulting. Nominate the direction the unit is jumping in and move it up to 2D6" in this direction. Any model finishing its move in impassable terrain is destroyed. If you roll a double, one member of the unit has been claimed by the Warp and is removed as a casualty (the survivors move up to the distance rolled, following the normal rules for jump infantry).

EXARCH WARGEAR

Spinneret Rifle: The spinneret rifle ejects a single rigid strand of monomolecular wire that punches through armour and recoils in a tight spiral. It has the following profile:

Range: 18"   S: 6   AP: 1   Assault 1, Pinning

Powerblades: Powerblades are twin power weapons fitted to the forearms, enabling the wearer to use both hands freely. Powerblades confer +1 A and ignore armour saves.

EXARCH POWERS

Surprise Assault: The Exarch and his squad teleport onto the battlefield in a crackling storm of light. He and his squad may always use the Deep Strike rule, regardless of the mission being played.

Withdraw: The Exarch watches the tides of combat closely for the best moment to withdraw from a fight, ready to attack again later. His unit has the Hit and Run special rule.

SHINING SPEARS

The Shining Spears are one of the rarest and most specialised aspects. They fight as the spear of Kaela Mensha Khaine, which struck like lightning and killed any foe with a single blow.

Shining Spears ride sleek, gleaming jetbikes to war, their vehicles' anti-gravitic motors allowing them to skim over even the roughest terrain at breakneck pace. Each Aspect Warrior is so in tune with his jetbike that he can execute complex high-speed aerial manoeuvres with a single gesture. Even a small unit of Shining Spears can turn the tide of a protracted combat, for their legendary charges hit home with the force of a thunderbolt.

The ritual armament of the aspect is the laser lance. This elegant weapon can deliver intense short ranged energy blasts, and is usually used just as the Shining Spears deliver their charge. The Aspect Warriors specialise in delivering hit-and-run attacks, careening past the foe and returning for another attack in much the same way as the duelling Dragon Knights of the Exodite worlds. Few enemies can withstand such a devastating charge.

	WS	BS	S	T	W	I	A	Ld	Sv
Shining Spear	4	4	3	3(4)	1	5	1	9	3+
Exarch	5	5	3	3(4)	1	6	2	9	3+

WARGEAR

Laser Lance: On any turn in which they initiate an assault, models armed with laser lances count as having Strength 6 power weapons. In addition they may be used as a ranged weapon with the following profile:

Range: 6"   S: 6   AP: 4   Assault 1, Lance

EXARCH WARGEAR

Star Lance: The star lance is an extremely powerful laser lance, named for the weapon wielded by Asuryan himself from the back of his flying steed. It follows the rules for a laser lance, but has a Strength of 8 in all cases.

EXARCH POWERS

Skilled Rider: The Exarch can lead his squad unerringly around tree trunks and branches, down twisting gorges and through rubble-strewn corridors. He and his squad have the Skilled Rider ability.

Withdraw: The Exarch watches the tides of combat closely for best moment to withdraw from a fight, ready to attack again later. His unit may use the Hit and Run special rule.

> "Trust not in their appearance, for the Eldar are as alien to good, honest men as the vile Tyranids and savage Orks. There is no understanding them for there is nothing to understand – they are a random force in the universe."
>
> **Imperial Commander Abriel Hume**

RANGERS

The Rangers of the Eldar are unparalleled scouts and expert marksmen. Although they adopt a nomadic lifestyle to escape the rigours of the Eldar path, most Outcasts remain loyal to their craftworlds and traditions. They take on the mantle of Ranger, and often choose to accept a mission from their Seers so that they can continue to serve their people in a useful fashion. Many die, alone and forgotten. Some fall from grace and become consumed by their dark passions, while others manage to exorcise their wanderlust and eventually return to their craftworld. They investigate alien planets, search for lost webway gates, explore new maiden worlds, and hunt down those who would harm their craftworlds. Sometimes Rangers are sent to recover lost artefacts, or retrieve the spirit stone from the corpse of a fallen warrior. Their greatest duty, however, is vigilance, keeping a close eye upon potential foes and reporting any source of danger to the craftworld.

Rangers wear a practical costume derived from the Exodite worlds, and can be recognised easily by their weather-beaten and well-travelled appearance. Most characteristic of all is the long chameleoline cloak they wear, a sophisticated but hard-wearing garment that allows a Ranger to merge seamlessly into the environment. In battle, a craftworld's Rangers will often gather into small groups to take up commanding positions on the battlefield. Blending in with their surroundings, they use their long rifles to deadly effect, their energy bolts finding the eye sockets and neck joints of even the most heavily armoured troops.

	WS	BS	S	T	W	I	A	Ld	Sv
Ranger	3	4	3	3	1	4	1	8	5+

SPECIAL RULES
Fleet of Foot.

Masters of Stealth: In the right circumstances, Rangers have the ability to work their way into a forward position on the battlefield. Rangers (and Pathfinders) have the Infiltrate, Move Through Cover and Stealth special rules.

Pathfinders: Some Rangers undertake permanent exile and become Pathfinders. Ranger squads that have been upgraded to Pathfinders may ignore difficult terrain. They have the Scouts special rule. Any cover save they use is improved by +2 instead of the usual +1 conferred by the Stealth rule.

WARGEAR
Ranger Long Rifle: The Ranger long rifle is a sniper rifle equipped with highly sophisticated sights. Any shooting roll to hit of a 6 counts as having AP 1. In a Pathfinder unit, any shooting roll to hit of 5+ counts as having AP 1.

Range: 36" S: X AP: 6 Heavy 1, Sniper, Pinning

> "The young do not desire the discipline of the Path, but rather their curiosity drives them to try every fruit from the tree. Thus it is that so many take the Path of Wandering or the Path of Damnation in their first years of adulthood, and so the great tragedy of our kind is played out again and again as the number of our people shrink from generation to generation."
>
> **Kysaduras the Anchorite,**
> **Introspections Upon Perfection**

GUARDIANS

Due to the gradual decline in the population of their race, the civilians of the Eldar are all too often forced to take up arms. Because of this, every Eldar is trained and ready to fight as a Guardian if need be. In some craftworlds the Guardians are the most common of all Eldar warriors. They are primarily a defence force, employed when a craftworld itself comes under threat, as the Aspect Warriors are often not numerous enough to overcome the hordes of the enemy without support.

Guardians wear a tight-fitting armoured suit consisting of thousands of tiny thermo-plastic cells woven together. Much like Aspect armour, when under the influence of blast pressure or gunshot these cells meld together into a rigid defence. This flexibility enables the Eldar Guardians unrestricted movement as they take up advantageous positions upon the battlefield.

The weapons used by the Guardians vary depending on battlefield role. Guardian Defenders act as support units, manning anti-grav heavy weapon platforms that glide effortlessly over even rugged terrain. If the enemy closes in on their position, the Guardians will unleash a hail of fire from their shuriken catapults. Guardian Storm squads are rare but effective, acting as assault troops in support of the craftworld's Aspect Warriors. It is a testament to the skill and technology of the Eldar that even their civilians are capable of engaging an enemy army and emerging victorious.

	WS	BS	S	T	W	I	A	Ld	Sv
Guardian	3	3	3	3	1	4	1	8	5+

SPECIAL RULES
Fleet of Foot.

WARGEAR
Guardian Heavy Weapon Platform: A heavy weapon mounted on a weapon platform counts as an assault weapon in all respects. It has two Guardians as crew, and must stay in coherency with at least one of the crew. Each crewman is armed with a shuriken catapult.

One crewman may fire the platform instead of his shuriken catapult, the other may shoot with his own weapon freely. Line of sight and range are always drawn from the firing crew member. If one crewman is killed the platform is operated as normal by the other crewman; if both crew are killed the platform is removed. The platform model itself is always ignored, including when measuring ranges to the unit, and when counting the number of models in the unit. It is essentially a marker; assume that the gun is actually carried by the crew member that is firing it.

THE GOD OF THE DEAD

A few Seers that have travelled along the most distant skeins of possible futures, Eldrad Ulthran foremost amongst them, see a hidden hope. They believe as more and more Eldar leave the mortal coil and become one with the infinity circuits, a new Eldar god grows in power – Ynnead, God of the Dead. They believe that when every last Eldar has died in the final days, Ynnead will awaken and have strength enough to defeat Slaanesh forever.

GUARDIAN JETBIKES

Eldar jetbikes are sleek one-man craft propelled by powerful anti-gravitic motors. Beautifully designed, the Eldar jetbike is a wonder of engineering. It is capable of such velocity that without the prodigious reaction speed of an Eldar it would be more lethal to the rider than his foe.

To an Eldar, the mastery of the jetbike is an exhilarating challenge. Jetbikes have long, curved vanes on either side that allow the rider to execute incredibly sharp turns in mid-air, and the strength of their anti-grav motors can be subtly manipulated to send the jetbikes hurtling into a steep dive or sharp climb. Even for an Eldar it takes years of practice to master a jetbike's potential, but one who does so builds a rapport with his steed comparable to the horsemasters of Eldar mythology.

Jetbike riders operate as forward scouts and fast-response strike forces, speeding across the battlefield in a brightly-coloured blur before unleashing tight fusillades from their hull-mounted shuriken weaponry. A common tactic for jetbike riders is to circumvent enemy lines completely and then close in on their vulnerable rear, taking a fearsome toll before gunning their engines and speeding off again.

"Feel the rush of the wind against your skin and hear her keening cry in your ears. Listen to her call well, for are we not the Wild Riders, the children of the storm?"

Nuadhu 'Fireheart'
chieftain of Saim-Hann

	WS	BS	S	T	W	I	A	Ld	Sv
Guardian Jetbike	3	3	3	3(4)	1	4	1	8	3+

WARGEAR

Eldar Jetbike: These are fitted with twin-linked shuriken catapults, increase the rider's Toughness by 1 point, and in addition confer a 3+ armour save to the rider. See the Warhammer 40,000 Rulebook for details of the movement of Eldar jetbikes.

VYPERS

The Eldar Vyper is an arrow-swift attack craft with a speed that belies its destructive potential. Originally pioneered by the artisans of the Saim-Hann craftworld, this light skimmer is designed to give fire support to fast-moving jetbike squadrons. Though lightly armoured, it is equipped with a weapon configuration comparable to a tank twice its size, and its sheer speed provides more surety against incoming fire than any amount of armour plating. The Vyper is piloted by two crew; one at the helm and one mounted in the gun nest at the rear. A Vyper crew usually share a bond that allows them to better coordinate their actions, and it is common to find that those manning a Vyper are blood relatives. A well-drilled Vyper squadron moves as one, and is capable of redeploying in seconds to find the vulnerable side or rear armour of an enemy tank or escape interceptors attempting to close with it. Notoriously reticent to close with the enemy, Vypers work best at range, harrying the outriders of the foe before boosting past them to pour yet more firepower into them from a new vantage point.

	Front Armour	Side Armour	Rear Armour	BS
Vyper	10	10	10	3

Type: Skimmer, Fast, Open-Topped

> "There is no art more beautiful and diverse as the art of death."
>
> **Laconfir of Biel-Tan**

FALCON

The Falcon is the primary battle tank of the Eldar army, its curved silhouette a familiar but much-dreaded sight to their enemies. During the war in heaven it was Faolchu, consort of the Great Hawk, who retrieved Vaul's mighty sword Anaris and gave it to the Eldar hero Eldanesh to aid his duel with Khaine. It is this principle of deliverance that is behind the design of the Falcon grav-tank. The Falcon has a twin role upon the field of battle. It has a passenger compartment enabling it to carry a small squad of fighters to the battlefront or rescue a beleaguered unit when resistance proves too fierce. It also carries a lethal assortment of heavy weaponry, and advanced targeters that allow it to fire devastating salvos whilst on the move. As with all Eldar tanks, the Falcon is held aloft by powerful anti-grav motors that allow it limited flight. Indeed, many Falcon pilots specialise in flying hidden within the clouds only to dive from the skies, pulse lasers and shuriken weapons spitting death into the ranks of the enemy.

THE WAR IN HEAVEN

The War in Heaven started by Khaine lasted for years, and there are many tales of the battles between the gods and the immortal demi-god giants called the Yngir. Gods changed sides, struck bargains and broke them, and the heavens shook to the fury of their fighting. Asuryan despaired of the destruction wrought by Khaine, and regretted his hasty anger with Kurnous and Isha. However, the Phoenix King refused to choose a side during the War in Heaven, and favoured neither Khaine nor the Children of Isha. Thus he wisely remained the lord of both.

	Front Armour	Side Armour	Rear Armour	BS
Falcon	12	12	10	3

Type: Tank, Fast, Skimmer

Transport: A Falcon may transport a single unit of infantry of up to 6 models.

Access points: 1 (rear access ramp)

Fire points: 0

Pulse Laser: The pulse laser sacrifices the penetrative power of the bright lance in return for a longer range and higher rate of fire.

Range: 48"   S: 8   AP: 2   Heavy 2

FIRE PRISM

Unlike the lumpen and unlovely battle tanks of other races, the Fire Prism is graceful and swift. Despite its aesthetic qualities the Fire Prism sacrifices none of the killing power associated with heavy armour, and its prism cannon is the bane of the heavy battle tanks of the crude races. The main armament of the Fire Prism is an extremely unusual device that uses a two-stage firing process. A medium-magnitude laser is discharged into a massive crystal prism that greatly amplifies the potency of the shot in a fraction of a second. This energy can be discharged in a focused beam capable of blasting through the thickest armour, or dispersed to slay entire squads of enemy infantry. Most unusual of all, sophisticated tracking arrays allow this technological wonder to channel its firepower through the prismatic lens of another prism cannon, forming one all-powerful laser blast that can obliterate any target.

	Front Armour	Side Armour	Rear Armour	BS
Fire Prism	12	12	10	4

Type: Tank, Fast, Skimmer

Prism Cannon: The prism cannon may be fired in a focussed or dispersed beam, using the following profile:

Focussed:

Range: 60"   S: 9   AP: 2   Heavy 1, Blast

Dispersed:

Range: 60"   S: 5   AP: 4   Heavy 1, Large Blast

If prism cannons have a line of sight to other prism cannons they may forfeit their chance to fire in order to combine beams. Pick one of the prism cannons as the firer, and the other(s) as contributor – the firing prism cannon's shot counts as twin-linked for that turn. Furthermore the strength of the shot is increased by 1 and the AP lowered by 1 for each cannon contributing to it. For example, if one Fire Prism contributes its beam to a second prism cannon, the beam the second prism cannon fires will be at S10 AP1 (focussed; the maximum Strength and AP) or S6 AP3 (dispersed).

ANARIS – THE SWORD OF DAWNLIGHT

In the last days of the War in Heaven, Vaul reforged the blade he had failed to finish for Khaine, and he made it the mightiest sword of all. He called it Anaris, which means dawnlight, and with this weapon in his hand he strode to do battle with the war god. The fight was long and Vaul did Khaine much injury, Anaris darted as swift and deadly as lightning, but in the end Khaine's fury overpowered the smith god and toppled him from heaven. It was as a result of this long battle that Vaul is said to have been crippled, and after Vaul's defeat Khaine chained him to his anvil and took Anaris for himself. Thus did the war god win the War in Heaven.

WAR WALKERS

Sacrificing armour in favour of hard-hitting weaponry and manoeuvrability, the graceful bipedal vehicle known as the War Walker is well suited to its role of scout. However, the pilot of a War Walker is not without protection, for the vehicle is equipped with an array of force fields that blur and distort its outline, making it at least as safe as a fully enclosed vehicle. Often the first thing an enemy will know about the presence of an Eldar force is a ripple in the terrain ahead followed by a blistering firestorm that efficiently eliminates the observer.

Being lightly built, squadrons of War Walkers rely on the use of their ranged weaponry to neutralise threats in order of priority. This is facilitated by extremely advanced support systems, including piloting failsafes in the form of spirit stones. It is said that during battle the pilot of a War Walker enters a kind of meditative state. He becomes one with his craft, the machine effortlessly stalking through terrain as its twin heavy weapons scythe through the foe. The sheer rate of fire a full squadron of War Walkers can provide is often enough to obliterate an entire platoon of enemy troops in a single volley.

	WS	BS	S	Front Armour	Side Armour	Rear Armour	I	A
War Walker	3	3	5	10	10	10	4	2

Type: Walker

SPECIAL RULES

Scouts: War Walkers are used for forward reconnaissance and hence have the Scouts rule.

VEHICLE UPGRADES

Eldar often adapt their vehicles for particular roles on the battlefield. Vehicles may choose these upgrades if allowed in their army list's entry.

Holo-field: The vehicle is surrounded by a shimmering holo-field that distorts its shape and prevents the enemy from targeting its most vulnerable locations. Whenever your opponent rolls on the damage table for that vehicle, they must roll two dice and apply the lowest result.

Spirit Stones: The vehicle incorporates a large spirit stone. The essence within it can control the vehicle for short periods of time should the crew be disabled. If the vehicle suffers a 'crew stunned' result it is automatically counted as a 'crew shaken' result.

Star Engines: The vehicle has a number of secondary engines that can be used to boost it to breakneck speeds. It may move an additional 12" in lieu of shooting, but troops may not embark or disembark that turn.

Vectored Engines: The vehicle can turn its engines to almost any angle, allowing the crew to circumvent disaster when damaged. If the vehicle would crash due to being immobilised, it instead makes a forced landing as if it had not moved that turn.

SUPPORT WEAPONS

Some Eldar Guardians operate sophisticated support weapon platforms that are much larger than those used by the Guardian Defenders. These gun batteries mount exotic artillery pieces to provide covering fire for the Aspect Warrior advance. Though the devastating weapons they carry are transported on anti-grav carriages, they are so large they must remain stationary to fire. This is offset by complex targeting arrays allowing them to pinpoint even the most well-hidden enemy troops.

	WS	BS	S	T	W	I	A	Ld	Sv
Guardian	3	3	3	3	1	4	1	8	5+

SPECIAL RULES

Artillery: Support weapons are artillery.

D-Cannon: The distort cannon, or D-cannon, uses the Eldar's advanced knowledge of Warp technology to unleash a miniature sphere of Warp energy onto the battlefield, tearing apart its targets. The D-cannon always wounds on a roll of 2+, and on a roll to wound of a 6 it inflicts instant death on the victim (regardless of its Toughness value). Against targets with an Armour Value, a D-cannon always inflicts a glancing hit on a roll of 3 or 4 and a penetrating hit on a roll of 5 or 6. It has the following profile:

   Range: G24"   S: X   AP: 2   Heavy 1, Blast

Vibro Cannon: A vibro cannon uses resonant sonic waves to shake its targets apart and fling troops to the ground. When firing a vibro cannon battery, roll to hit (the firer does not need to pick a target). If any of the vibro cannons hit, draw a single 36" line from one vibro cannon in any direction. Any unit which the line passes through suffers D6 hits. For each vibro cannon in the battery after the first, add 1 to the strength of these hits. For example, a unit of three vibro cannons rolls a 1, a 6 and a 4 to hit; they would draw a single line from one of the cannon and any unit it touches takes D6 S6 hits.

A target with an Armour Value that is hit by a vibro cannon always suffers a single glancing hit; do not roll for armour penetration.

   Range: 36"   S: 4   AP: –   Heavy 1, Pinning

Shadow Weaver: The shadow weaver unleashes a cloud of razor-sharp monofilament wire high into the air, which drifts down onto the enemy, slicing through the flesh and bones of the targets as they struggle to free themselves. It has the following profile:

   Range: G48"   S: 6   AP: –   Heavy 1, Blast

WAVE SERPENT

The Wave Serpent is the main troop carrier of a craftworld's army. Protected inside its sleek hull, strike forces of Aspect Warriors and Guardians can be transported in safety to any part of the battlefield. The Wave Serpent's energy field projectors generate a rippling bow wave of force at the front of the craft that disrupts incoming fire. Its powerful anti-grav engines give it speed enough to hurtle across a battlefield in seconds. These abilities, combined with superior heavy weaponry, make the Wave Serpent a superb asset to the Eldar warhost in all theatres of war.

	Front Armour	Side Armour	Rear Armour	BS
Wave Serpent	12	12	10	3

Type: Tank, Fast, Skimmer

Transport: A Wave Serpent may transport a single unit of infantry of up to 12 models (or 5 Wraithguard models and up to two characters).

Access points: 1 (rear access ramp)

Fire points: 0

SPECIAL RULES

Energy Field: The prow of a Wave Serpent is protected by an energy field to ward off enemy shots. Any ranged attack against the Wave Serpent from the front or side arc with a Strength of greater than 8 counts as S8. In addition, all ranged attacks never roll more than +1D6 for their armour penetration (for example, melta weapons at half range or ordnance only roll one dice). Attacks in close combat, or from the rear, are unaffected by the energy field rule.

WRAITHGUARD

To the Eldar, death does not guarantee respite from war. With the guidance of a Seer, it is possible for an Eldar spirit to separate itself from the infinity circuit and flow into a spirit stone put aside for that purpose. Such a spirit stone can then be placed within the robotic body of a wraith-construct, imbuing its artificial form with a living intellect. Though this process is abhorrent to the Eldar, none can deny that the resultant combination of fierce warrior spirit and impervious host body is a major weapon in the Eldar arsenal.

The predominant type of ghost warrior is the Wraithguard. These are entirely constructed from the resilient psychoplastic wraithbone, and tower above the Warlocks that accompany them upon the battlefield. They have the same exquisite design and flowing organic shapes common to all Eldar

constructs. However these wraith-constructs contrast sharply with their living counterparts, for the vitality and alacrity of the Eldar is absent. Instead the Wraithguard stride purposefully forward with the inevitability of death, the sepulchral silence of their advance punctuated only by the sound of reality itself being torn apart by their wraithcannon.

Too heavy for a normal Eldar to carry, the wraithcannon allows a Wraithguard to focus a portion of its psychic power upon a fixed point. This incredible weapon can then open a rift between Warp space and the material universe at that location for a split second. If this rift is opened within an enemy, the results range from catastrophic trauma to full bodily displacement into the depths of the Warp. It is best not to dwell on the fate of such unfortunate individuals.

	WS	BS	S	T	W	I	A	Ld	Sv
Wraithguard	4	4	5	6	1	4	1	10	3+

SPECIAL RULES

Fearless: Wraithguard are not living creatures and are therefore not affected by emotions such as dread and urges of self-preservation. They are Fearless, and confer this ability to any characters joining them.

Wraithsight: Wraithguard do not see the world as mortals do, but instead witness an ever-shifting image of spirits that makes them slower to react to changes on the battlefield. At the start of their turn, roll a D6 for each Wraithguard unit that is not within 6" of a friendly psyker. On a roll of a 1, the Wraithguard is inactive until the end of their turn. Inactive models may not move, shoot, assault or attack in close combat, and are hit automatically in close combat.

WARGEAR

Wraithcannon: The wraithcannon works by opening a small Warp space/real space hole, tearing apart the target as it is ripped between dimensions. The wraithcannon always wounds on a roll of 2+, and a roll to wound of a 6 it inflicts instant death on the victim (regardless of its Toughness value). Against targets with an Armour Value, a wraithcannon always inflicts a glancing hit on a roll of 3 or 4 and a penetrating hit on a roll of 5 or 6. It has the following profile:

Range: 12"   S: X   AP: 2   Assault 1

"The universe is tripartite: the sunlight of the material plane, the darkness of the spirit plane, and the twilight of the spaces betwixt the two."

Spiritseer Iyanna Arienal

WRAITHLORD

Wraithlords are graceful but mighty wraith-nobles that dwarf even their Wraithguard cousins. These statuesque constructs are extremely precious to their craftworlds and have a supernatural toughness due to their wraithbone construction. Summoned into being by the necromantic processes of the Spiritseers, only a true hero of the Eldar race has spirit enough to animate the gigantic wraithbone shell of a Wraithlord.

The consciousness of the dead is never fully as individual or alert as that of the living. It exists at once in the real world and the spiritual world of the Warp, and moves through reality as in a dream where thought and feelings are as tangible as steel and stone. Despite this, Wraithlords are sometimes

summoned for a council of war, for they can communicate telepathically and invariably have millennia of experience.

There are many different forms of Wraithlord, most of which have been pioneered by craftworld Iyanden to better the suit the warrior spirit inside. If the animating force within the Wraithlord specialised in close assault when it was alive, it will seek to tear apart its enemies with great energised fists or cleave several apart with a swing from its wraithblade. If it specialised in support, the ghost warrior's energy core will instead be rerouted to power a devastating array of heavy weaponry. Either way, a single Wraithlord can turn the tide of battle; the legends of the fallen heroes within continuing to grow even in death.

	WS	BS	S	T	W	I	A	Ld	Sv
Wraithlord	4	4	10	8	3	4	2	10	3+

SPECIAL RULES

Fearless: Wraithlords are not living creatures and are therefore not affected by emotions such as dread and urges of self-preservation. They are Fearless.

Monstrous Creature: Wraithlords are monstrous creatures.

Wraithsight: Wraithlords see the world as an ever-shifting image of spirits that makes them slower to react to changes on the battlefield. At the start of its own turn, roll a D6 for each Wraithlord that is not within 6" of a friendly psyker. On a roll of a 1, the Wraithlord is inactive until the end of its turn. Inactive models may not move, shoot, assault or attack in close combat, and are hit automatically in close combat.

WARGEAR

Wraithblade: A wraithblade has a sentience unto itself and guides the wielder's blows. It allows the Wraithlord to re-roll failed rolls to hit in close combat.

THE ELDAR MOONS

Although the whereabouts of the original Eldar homeworld is unknown, it is said that this world had three moons. These were called Lileath the Maiden Moon that was purest white, Kurnous the Hunter's Moon that was greenish and dim, and Eldanesh the Red Moon. When Khaine slew Eldanesh the dead Eldar Lord was set into the sky, and the colour red was a constant reminder of his bloody death. Even today Eldar regard the emblem of the red moon as a portent of disaster.

HARLEQUINS

For the warrior dancers of the Harlequins, there is no distinction between art and war. Followers of the cunning deity known as the Laughing God, they are the strangest and most inscrutable of all the Eldar. Their mastery of the physical arts twinned with their incredible speed makes the Harlequins the deadliest fighters of their race. Every moment is a performance, and they perform their legendary masques with puissant skill, flair and passion – their hallmark upon the field of battle.

The Harlequins are not tied to any particular craftworld but wander from world to world through the interspatial tunnels of the webway. They occasionally grace other Eldar with impressive performances and acrobatic displays, and are even rumoured to visit the cursed Dark Eldar in their twilight city of Commorragh. In these pageants each Harlequin plays the role of one of the figures from Eldar legend, and they act out stylised versions of Eldar mythic cycles.

Harlequins wear exotic multi-coloured costumes at all times, and employ shimmering holo-suits they call dathedi. Similar in function to the holo-fields used by Eldar battle tanks, a holo-suit breaks up the outline of the wearer. Every time the wearer moves his outline explodes into a scintillating cloud of tiny fragments, and when he stops he image coalesces into a solid image once again. The Harlequins never show their real faces but conceal them beneath a shifting mask that can assume any image at the will of the wearer. When the followers of the Laughing God go to war, their masks reflect the worst nightmares of those who gaze upon them.

	WS	BS	S	T	W	I	A	Ld	Sv
Harlequin	5	4	3	3	1	6	2	9	–
Shadowseer	5	4	3	3	1	6	2	9	–
Death Jester	5	4	3	3	1	6	2	9	–
Troupe Master	5	4	3	3	1	6	3	10	–

SPECIAL RULES
Fleet of Foot.

Dance of Death: A Harlequin troupe coordinates its attacks with bewildering speed, dancing through the enemy ranks, leaving corpses in their wake. They have the Furious Assault and the Hit and Run special rules.

WARGEAR
Flip Belts: The anti-gravity flip belts of the Harlequins enable them to dart through the roughest terrain with their feet barely touching the ground. They ignore difficult terrain.

Holo-suit: Harlequins use a sophisticated holo-suit to fragment their image and foil incoming fire and blows from their enemies. They benefit from a 5+ invulnerable save.

Harlequin's Kiss: A sharpened tube attached to the forearm, the Kiss can be punched into an enemy and the monofilament wire inside allowed to uncoil, reducing the target's insides to a gory soup in an instant. A Harlequin's Kiss counts as a close combat weapon. In addition, close combat attacks made by a model armed with a Harlequin's Kiss have the Rending special rule.

Fusion Pistol: This compact hand-held melta weapon has an elegance that belies its potency. It has the following profile:

Range: 6" S: 8 AP: 1 Pistol, Melta

SHADOWSEERS

Shadowseers are specialist psykers whose abilities are centred around confusion and fear. They add to the potency of their performances by releasing programmed hallucinations from their *creidann* grenade launcher backpacks. During the masques, the Shadowseers act as storytellers, forming scintillating phantoms that dance and duel in the air. In battle, they can force visions of unholy terror upon the foe or even remove the Harlequin's presence from their minds altogether.

Hallucinogen Grenades: The Shadowseer's entire squad counts as armed with plasma grenades.

Veil of Tears: A Shadowseer is a psyker and always has the Veil of Tears psychic power. It follows the same rules as Warlock powers (see page 20-21).

The Shadowseer uses her powers to confuse and terrify her foe. Any enemy unit wishing to target the Shadowseer or the unit she is with must roll 2D6x2. This is their spotting distance in inches.

If the models are not within spotting range, they may not fire that turn. The Shadowseer and her unit can always be ignored by the enemy for the purpose of determining target priority.

THE DANCE WITHOUT END

The plays and songs of the Harlequins are full of subtle meanings and significances that only the Eldar can fully appreciate. The roles within each performance are always taken by the same players, thus the role of the Laughing God is always played by the Troupe Master himself, whilst that of Fate is played by the Shadowseer, Death by the Death Jester and so on. The majority of roles are played by the Chorus and the Mimes, who make up the bulk of the Troupe. Having no individual names or identities they have become the players of the Troupe in a quite literal way. For example, Mimes never speak and always wear their expressive shape-shifting masks, never revealing their faces.

Only one can play the part of She Who Thirsts – the silent and reclusive Harlequin known as the Solitaire. His role commands ultimate fear and respect, and also makes him the most dangerous of all Harlequins, for a Solitaire treads the Path of Damnation.

DEATH JESTERS

The Death Jesters are heavy weapon specialists, sinister warriors who stand apart from their fellow Harlequins and even from each other. Their costumes always feature skulls, bones and death's head masks, and are often decorated with bones of their predecessors. Death Jesters have a morbid sense of humour, and their mocking laugh often heralds a messy and painful death.

Shrieker Cannon: A Death Jester's shrieker cannon fires shuriken impregnated with virulent genetic toxins, causing its victims to rupture and explode in spectacular fashion. It has the following profile:

Range: 24"   S: 6   AP: 5   Assault 3, Pinning

ELDRAD ULTHRAN
FARSEER OF ULTHWÉ

Chief amongst the Farseers of Ulthwé was Eldrad Ulthran. Eldrad lived for a great many centuries, and successfully guided his people along the twisting paths of fate. It was his prognostications that resulted in the armies of Ulthwé moving suddenly and unexpectedly against the Orks of the Warlord Ghazghkull Thraka's homeworld. As a result of Eldar raids, the balance of power amongst rival factions was changed to favour Ghazghkull rather than another Ork Warlord whose ambitions were more directly perilous to the Eldar. As a consequence it was the Human world of Armageddon that felt the full wrath of Ghazghkull's Waaagh! Neither Orks nor Humans ever suspected that this was the fulfilment of Eldrad's deliberate policy to direct Orkish aggression away from the craftworlds. Such is the way that the Farseers manipulate the time-stream, with great skill and subtlety, without ever raising the suspicion of other races.

Time and time again, Eldrad averted disaster for the Eldar race, acts of subtle heroism hidden within severed strands of fate. It was Eldrad who prevented the Hrud infestation of proud Saim-Hann that would otherwise have reduced it to rotting mulch. It was Eldrad who thwarted the malefic works of the newly-risen Necron gods, and who stopped the Days of Blood from coming to pass.

The most important prediction of Eldrad Ulthran concerned the sudden opening of the massive Warp-space rift that preluded the many battles on the Exodite world of Haran. Ulthran foretold how the Chaos gods would force a great rupture in space, creating a hole through which the forces of Chaos could pour into the universe. Why Haran rather than any other world was difficult to guess, but it may be that the minions of the Chaos gods planned to infiltrate the webway from Haran, using the Warp-tunnels to reach other planets and craftworlds.

THE DOME OF CRYSTAL SEERS
As Farseers grow older their minds become so closely linked with the wraithbone core of their craftworld that their physical bodies grow dormant. Eventually a Farseer of great age will retreat to the Dome of Crystal Seers. Here the ship's wraithbone core breaks into a broad bio-dome where groves of wraithbone trees reach out into space. Inside the dome the Farseer's body gradually crystallises and takes root, until eventually he turns entirely to crystal. His spirit is freed into the craftworld itself, preserved forever within the psycho-conductive wraithbone infinity circuit. Other Eldar sometimes wander through the Dome of Crystal Seers to look upon the Farseers of old whose forms are preserved forever amongst the glades of wraithbone trees.

When the rift opened the Eldar were prepared. Chaos Space Marines joined the daemons that poured through the rift and battles raged across the planet. The Eldar forces were mustered in strength, but could barely contain the forces of Chaos. Eldrad himself led the warriors of Ulthwé. From all over the galaxy came Phoenix Lords and Outcasts to fight for the Eldar cause. The rift grew bigger as more daemons infiltrated the world, but as the Eldar destroyed them the rift began to close. The war for Haran went on for many long months. Sometimes Chaos won the upper hand and the rift threatened to engulf the entire planet, becoming a permanent Warp-real space overlap. At other times the Eldar pushed back the forces of Chaos and the rift almost closed, banishing the daemons forever. Eventually, the Eldar triumphed, though at terrible cost, and Haran was denied to Chaos. The planet was known thereafter known as Haranshemash, the world of blood and tears.

In later years Eldrad became immensely resilient and very powerful. Like many of the most ancient Farseers he grew apart from the world of flesh and blood, and spent long days in the Dome of Crystal Seers. But Eldrad's works seem doomed to go unfinished. In the desperate days of the Despoiler's Thirteenth Black Crusade, Eldrad coordinated Ulthwé's defences. He poured his consciousness into many waystones, passing them to his lieutenants to guide his craftworld's war. The ancient Farseer led a foray into Abaddon's greatest weapon-ship: a twisted and prehistoric Blackstone Fortress that was poised to destroy the Human world of Cadia. In a desperate attempt to stop it opening a massive gateway to the Warp, Eldrad entered the Blackstone Fortress's psychic matrix and pitted his spirit against its corrupted heart. In that instant his mortal body was gone, and all but a handful of his waystones became lifeless and dull.

In this last great act Eldrad passed into the half-light of Eldar legend. He has become a figure synonymous with wisdom, foresight and self-sacrifice. Only the youngest of Eldrad's protégés, Q'sandria, believes that the Farseer can survive his unending struggle within the heart of the Chaos fleet. For how can a single soul be strong enough to escape the predations of the Warp?

ELDRAD ULTHRAN

	WS	BS	S	T	W	I	A	Ld	Sv
Eldrad	5	5	3	4	3	5	1	10	–

SPECIAL RULES

Independent Character.

Psychic Powers: Eldrad is a psyker and has the Eldritch Storm, Fortune, Guide, Doom and Mind War psychic powers.

Divination: Eldrad's powers of precognition and prophecy are legendary. After both sides have deployed at the start of a game, the Eldar player may reposition D3+1 units in his army. No unit may be moved outside of its deployment zone.

WARGEAR

Shuriken pistol, witchblade, runes of warding, runes of witnessing, ghosthelm, spirit stones.

Rune armour: 3+ invulnerable save.

Staff of Ulthamar: This potent artefact can channel Eldrad's immense psychic powers through the staff, or be used as a powerful weapon. If Eldrad is not in an assault it can allow Eldrad to use a third psychic power per turn, which may be a psychic power he has already used that turn. In combat it always wounds on a roll of 2+ and ignores armour saves.

PSYCHIC RUNES

An Eldar Seer controls his powers by means of psycho-receptive wraithbone runes. These runes are secreted about the Farseer's person, and function like keys, locking and unlocking the power of the Eldar's mind as well as safeguarding it from the perils of the Warp. Different rune shapes represent different powers and states of mind. The more experienced a Seer becomes the more runes he can use. The most ancient of Seers may even make new runes of their own and teach others how to use them.

Runes enable a Seer to draw power from the Warp. By using the runes to focus the raw energies of the Warp, the Seer avoids serious danger. If he draws too much or attempts a task beyond him the rune glows hot and, if the Seer persists, is destroyed. Only if he attempts to utilise a rune that he has not fully mastered is the Seer in peril.

It is said that the spirits of ancient Seers flow between a craftworld's infinity circuit and the runes of its Seers. Thus the power of the infinity circuit lies behind the runic powers, and the spirits of the dead continue to guide the living along the Path of the Seer. This is why the Seers sometimes refer to the guiding spirits that assist them, meaning the ancient Seers whose sage advice comes to them through their runes.

As his powers develop a Seer will usually favour some aspect of his art. Some develop their kinetic powers and use them to create living symphonies of shape and movement. Others learn how to use their empathic powers to heal and counsel, and they assume the roles of doctors and advisors. Still others become tacticians and strategists, whose role is to safeguard the craftworld's future.

PRINCE YRIEL
AUTARCH OF IYANDEN

Autarch of Iyanden, High Admiral of the Eldritch Raiders and bastard scion of the House of Ulthanash, Prince Yriel is a consummate Eldar commander. He has led his forces to countless victories without fail both on the battlefield and in the darkness of space. It was his fleet that annihilated the Chaos armada during the Battle of the Burning Moon. It was his fleet that vanquished the repulsive bio-ships of Hive Fleet *Kraken* and saved Iyanden, though in doing so, Yriel has doomed himself to a slow and terrible death.

Over fifty years before the Tyranid assault, Yriel led the grand fleet of his craftworld. Though not of pure Iyanden blood, he was the pride of his craftworld and was widely considered the greatest genius to have ever sailed the void. Yriel's character was flawed not only in bloodline, however, but also by the sin of pride.

When Iyanden was threatened by an encroaching Chaos fleet, Yriel led the entire navy in a devastating pre-emptive attack that destroyed the foe, but in the process left Iyanden unprotected. Yriel expected to be honoured for his victory, but on his return he was stripped of rank for his recklessness. Furious, he vowed that he would never set foot upon Iyanden again. He became Outcast and led his followers into exile as a Corsair Prince. Such was his talent and drive that, within a few short decades, Yriel's Eldritch Raiders had become the most feared Corsair fleet in the galaxy.

When the claws of Hive Fleet *Kraken* began to dig deep into Iyanden's defences, the craftworld's Farseers bitterly regretted the disappearance of their navy's greatest asset. The sheer scale of the bio-ship invasion alone was enough to drown all hope. As tides of alien killers began to infest the craftworld itself, all believed the end was nigh. The flame of Iyanden's defiance was all but snuffed out.

Just as the Eldar reached the point of total despair, salvation came from the heavens. Cutting his way through the cordon of misshapen hive ships, Yriel and his Raiders swept to the aid of their people. His return tipped the balance of the epic conflict between the two fleets, and despite the horrendous losses suffered by the Eldar, the hive fleet was ultimately destroyed.

The final battle did not take place amongst the stars. Yriel took the fight to the Tyranids upon shattered Iyanden itself, seeking to personally slay the leader of the swarms – a monster so formidable it could not be killed by mortal weaponry. To the horror of the craftworld's Farseers, Yriel took the cursed Spear of Twilight from its stasis field in the Shrine of Ulthanash: an ancient weapon so powerful it would burn the bearer's soul. With the eldritch artefact blazing in his grasp, Yriel slaughtered his way to the Tyranid leader-beast. As he drove the Spear of Twilight through the creature's massive armoured head, its death scream signalled defeat for the Tyranid hordes.

Yriel was later restored to Admiralship of Iyanden's fleet, but in saving his people he had doomed himself, for the Spear is no normal weapon and cannot be abandoned. Though he holds the office of Autarch to this day, he still plies the stars, seeking a way to restore his craftworld to its former glory before he finally fades into myth.

CORSAIRS

There are many Eldar Corsairs whose names have become infamous throughout the Eldar craftworlds and beyond. Some of these are bloodthirsty individuals who fall prey to the same weaknesses of character that led to the Fall. Galadhar the Grey was one whose bloody deeds will live forever in the memories of the people of Duro. This was the Exodite world that he used as a base and from which he plundered a hundred worlds, murdering on a whim and devastating whole cities without a single qualm. His vicious exploits eventually brought doom to Duro as the Imperium hunted down Galadhar, bringing fire and death to the once peaceful world before Galadhar's ship was eventually destroyed.

Yet sometimes an Eldar Corsair may display the greatest compassion to their defeated enemies if it pleases them to do so. The so-called Duke of Asteri Reach, Avele Swifteye, commands a Corsair fleet out of Biel-Tan craftworld, and has continued Biel-Tan's pledge to protect the Maiden worlds from settlement by lesser races. On the world of Yrthal, Avele destroyed half a dozen Human settlements before the fledgling Imperial colony surrendered. He took the surviving forty thousand colonists to a nearby habitable moon, keeping them in stasis aboard his ships while they shuttled back and forth in short warp jumps, and promised that no further hostilities would be taken against them if they did not stray back to Yrthal.

PRINCE YRIEL OF IYANDEN

	WS	BS	S	T	W	I	A	Ld	Sv
Yriel	6	6	3	3	3	7	4	10	3+

SPECIAL RULES

Independent Character, Fleet of Foot.

Master Strategist: Like all Autarchs, Yriel is a superb commander. He has the Master Strategist rule (p.18).

Doomed: Yriel is constantly battling to stop the energies of the Spear of Twilight from consuming him, his forceshield allaying the worst of the weapon's effects. At the end of every game, Yriel suffers one automatic wound from his own weapon. Yriel may take his forceshield save as normal.

WARGEAR

Forceshield: 4+ invulnerable save.

Plasma grenades.

The Spear of Twilight: Yriel is eternally bound to the Spear of Twilight, Cursed Blade of the House of Ulthanash; a weapon that is said to contain the baleful energies of a dying sun. It is a singing spear that ignores armour saves (see page 27).

The Eye of Wrath: Yriel sports a monocular device over his left eye that can unleash a tempest of lightning upon those under his gaze. Once per game, Yriel can activate the Eye of Wrath in lieu of making his normal attacks in assault. Place the large blast template with the hole centred over Yriel; all models under the template take a Strength 6 hit at AP 3. Yriel is not affected.

> "Ask not the Eldar a question, for they will give you three answers, all of which are true and terrifying to know."
>
> **Inquisitor Czevak**

THE PHOENIX LORDS

The Phoenix Lords are demigods of battle whose legends span the stars, the most ancient of the Eldar Exarchs. They are the embodiments of the Warrior, as the Avatar is the incarnation of the Bloody-handed God Kaela Mensha Khaine.

Of all the Phoenix Lords the oldest is Asurmen, whose name means the Hand of Asuryan. Asurmen is also known as the Hand of the Phoenix King, for he acts as the immortal scion of Asuryan, father and chief of all the Eldar gods. In the time of the Fall, Asurmen led his people into exile, abandoning his world to the horrors of the Warp. He founded the first of the Aspect Warrior shrines, the Shrine of Asur, upon the barren world his people settled. From the Shrine of Asur sprang the first Aspect Warriors, and the Path of the Warrior was opened for the very first time. Those Eldar learned well at the feet of their master and in their turn they assumed the mantle of Exarchs, spreading their own teachings throughout the galaxy.

The first Exarchs, the Asurya, founded the shrines of the Warrior Aspects as the Eldar know them today. It was then that the first of the Warrior Aspects were formalised, taking as a model the skills and specialities of their founders. Great shrines were built on the craftworlds as they took to deep space so the warrior skills of the Asurya were preserved as their children began an eternity of exile.

Like the Exarchs of the Warrior Aspects, the Phoenix Lords are immortal after a fashion. When one of the Phoenix Lords dies, another Eldar dons his armour to take his place and thus his identity. In this way, should a Phoenix Lord be vanquished, they are ultimately reborn into a fresh cycle of existence. No matter how many individuals a Phoenix Lord may have been, their mind is forever the same, driven by the dominant personality of the first and greatest to wear the suit.

Unlike the Exarchs of the craftworlds, the Phoenix Lords are not bound to a single place, but roam across the galaxy. Once, long ago, they were worshipped as gods within their own shrines, but now these are long gone. In time their worlds were destroyed, or else overtaken with disaster. Today, the Aspect Warriors still nurture the many stories of the Asurya's heroic deeds, for they live not only in legend but in reality. Often a Phoenix Lord will vanish for centuries, or millennia, only to reappear at times of need, following the path of the Bloody-handed God across the universe.

THE CRONE WORLDS

The worlds that were consumed by the Eye of Terror still exist today, half real and half part of the Warp. In this environment both daemons and mortals can survive, and the physical laws of the material universe intermix with the endless possibilities of Chaos to produce hellish nightmare planets. It is impossible to imagine more vile or outlandish places, where the skies burn with fire, rivers run with blood, and mortals are driven to torment by their daemonic masters. Every world is a hell whose form is a creation of a mighty Daemon Prince, the most favoured servants of the Chaos gods.

To the Eldar these worlds are known as the crone worlds. According to tradition the crone worlds still preserve some of the Eldar's greatest treasures despite the changes that Chaos has wrought upon them. It is said that there are worlds where Eldar still live. Eldar Outcasts sometimes quest for these worlds, searching for some lost treasure or friend. They rarely return and those that do are often so badly wounded in mind and spirit that they soon seek the solace of the infinity circuits.

PHOENIX LORD

	WS	BS	S	T	W	I	A	Ld	Sv
Phoenix Lord	7	7	4	4	3	7	4	10	2+

SPECIAL RULES

In addition to the individual special rules listed in their entries on the following pages, all Phoenix Lords have the following special rules:

Independent Character.

Fleet of Foot: All Phoenix Lords are Fleet of Foot, regardless of Aspect.

Fearless: Having travelled the galaxy for millennia, Phoenix Lords are Fearless.

Eternal Warriors: Phoenix Lords can never truly be destroyed, and are hence immune to the effects of the Instant Death rule.

Disciples: Phoenix Lords typically lead their brethren into battle. If the Phoenix Lord is leading a squad of their Aspect, then the whole squad becomes Fearless. Phoenix Lords cannot join Aspect Warrior squads that are not of their Aspect. Note that if a squad has two of the same Exarch power, they are not cumulative.

ASURMEN, THE HAND OF ASURYAN

Asurmen, first of the Dire Avengers, founded more shrines on more craftworlds than any other Phoenix Lord. Soon after their inception he vanished, but tales of his deeds persisted. He was reported fighting against the Great Enemy from the Eye of Terror to the galaxy's rim, and word of his valour spread.

Asurmen's armour is fitted with a special shuriken weapon connected to each of his vambraces in such a way that it can be fired either-handed without loss of accuracy. This arrangement also leaves his hand free so that he can grasp his power sword with two hands. This itself is no ordinary power sword but the potent Sword of Asur. This diresword, the first of its kind, contains the spirit stone of Asurmen's brother Tethesis, that he may continue the fight against the minions of the Great Enemy until the end of time.

Aspect: Dire Avengers.

Wargear: Wrist-mounted Avenger shuriken catapults (as an Avenger shuriken catapult but with Assault 4), the Sword of Asur. The Sword of Asur is a diresword that allows Asurmen to re-roll misses in close combat.

Warrior Powers: Asurmen has the Defend and Bladestorm Exarch powers.

Battle Fate: Asurmen is destined to an existence of unending war from which there is no respite. He has a 4+ invulnerable save.

JAIN ZAR, THE STORM OF SILENCE

When Asurmen raised the first Aspect Warriors he selected Jain Zar for her speed and ferocity, and she became the first of the Asurya. Jain Zar travelled the webway, teaching her warrior skills to the Eldar, and leading others along the Warrior Path. Soon there were shrines to the Howling Banshees on all the large craftworlds, and many Exarchs to teach the warrior skills of Jain Zar to future generations.

Of all the Phoenix Lords, Jain Zar is the most devoted to the shrines of the Warrior Aspects throughout the craftworlds. She travels the webway, visiting the shrines and nurturing her spiritual descendants. Although she might disappear for centuries at a time, she always returns, and the shrines maintain a vigil for their deadly mistress.

Her astonishing speed and mercurial temperament is echoed by each of her Howling Banshee daughters, and it was she who first mastered the Scream that Steals. Jain Zar wields the deadly Blade of Destruction and the Jainas Mor, the Silent Death –

a triple-bladed throwing weapon that always returns to her hand in a glittering arc.

Aspect: Howling Banshees

Wargear: Banshee mask, executioner, the Silent Death. The Silent Death is a triskele with S5.

Warrior Powers: Jain Zar has the Acrobatic and War Shout Exarch powers.

Furious Charge: Specialising in devastating assaults, Jain Zar is a terrifying sight when leaping into battle. She has the Furious Charge special rule.

THE ASURYATA

The Asuryata, the legend of the Phoenix Lords, is an ancient epic known in full only to the Bards of Twilight. Its final stanzas speak of the Rhana Dandra, a star-spanning apocalypse that sees the final death of the Eldar and their gods alike.

BAHARROTH, THE CRY OF THE WIND

Baharroth is the oldest of the Swooping Hawks, the first of the winged Exarchs, and the founder of the Warrior Path that is represented today by Swooping Hawk shrines throughout the craftworlds. He was the most vibrant and youthful of the Phoenix Lords, revelling in the sensation of the sun on his wings. Baharroth and Maugan Ra are brothers as the sun is to the moon, and many of the Eldar's deadliest foes have found their doom on the edge of their blades. Since learning the arts of war from Asurmen himself, Baharroth has been reborn many times. Innumerable battlefields have felt his anger. Countless foes have fallen before his might.

Baharroth means the Cry of the Wind, for he is the master of flight and though he moves with the subtlety of a zephyr he attacks with the force of a hurricane.

It is said that his final death will come fighting alongside the other Phoenix Lords at the Rhana Dandra – the battle between Chaos and the material universe that will end with the destruction of both.

Aspect: Swooping Hawks

Wargear: Swooping Hawk wings, Swooping Hawk grenade pack, plasma grenades, haywire grenades, power weapon, hawk's talon.

Warrior Powers: Baharroth has the Intercept and Skyleap Exarch powers.

Hit and Run: Baharroth is able to dart from the blades of his foes and attack again in the blink of an eye. He has the Hit and Run rule (this ability is conferred to any unit of Swooping Hawks that Baharroth joins).

KARANDRAS, THE SHADOW HUNTER

Karandras is the most mysterious of the Phoenix Lords. No one knows where his shrine originally lay, but perhaps it was on one of the many small craftworlds that survived the Fall but were destroyed soon after. He is not the oldest of the Exarchs of the Striking Scorpions, for that honour belongs to Arhra the Father of Scorpions, the most sinister of all the Phoenix Lords, the Fallen Phoenix who burns with the dark light of Chaos. Karandras took his place, tempering the murderous nature of his predecessor with the patience of the hunter.

Karandras has the most potent sting of any Striking Scorpion, and uses claw and blade to rip his opponents to shreds before they are even aware of his presence. The mandiblasters used by Karandras, known as the Scorpion's Bite, are many times more powerful than those used by the Striking Scorpion Aspect Warriors. Few have set eyes upon Karandras and lived to tell the tale.

Aspect: Striking Scorpions

Wargear: The Scorpion's Bite, scorpion chainsword, scorpion's claw, plasma grenades. The Scorpion's Bite is a powerful mandiblaster that confers +2 attacks instead of +1.

Warrior Powers: Karandras has the Shadowstrike and Stalker Exarch powers.

Stealth: Karandras is able to draw the shadows around himself when creeping closer to his prey. He has the Stealth special rule (this ability is conferred to any unit of Striking Scorpions Karandras joins).

FUEGAN, THE BURNING LANCE

Fuegan learned the arts of war in the Shrine of Asur, in the distant time when the Warrior Aspects were born. Fuegan founded the shrines of the Fire Dragons, and schooled them in the art of war with fire and flame. Legend has it that Fuegan refused to flee when the Shrine of Asur was destroyed by the Fallen Phoenix, and was thought lost until he reappeared at the last battle of Haranshemash, the world of blood and tears. After that conflict Fuegan vanished into the webway, and has travelled its secret tunnels ever since, tracking down the enemies of his ancient forebears.

It is said Fuegan will call together the Phoenix Lords for the Rhana Dandra, and that he will be the last to die in that final conflict. Fuegan is armed with a massive and deadly firepike, and carries the Fire Axe.

This ancient weapon glows red with the heat of its forging. It has never cooled since the day it was made, and the runes upon its surface writhe in fiery agony.

Aspect: Fire Dragons

Wargear: Firepike, the Fire Axe, melta bombs. The Fire Axe confers +1S to his attacks and allows Fuegan to attack as a monstrous creature (ignores armour saves, rolls 2D6+5 for armour penetration).

Warrior Powers: Fuegan has the Tank Hunter and Crack Shot Exarch powers.

Feel No Pain: Fuegan can walk through a raging inferno without coming to harm. He has the Feel No Pain special rule.

MAUGAN RA,
THE HARVESTER OF SOULS

Altansar was one of the many craftworlds, both large and small, that survived the Fall. It rode out the psychic shock-waves that destroyed the Eldar realms but was subsequently caught in the gravity well of the Eye of Terror. Although the Eldar of Altansar fought valiantly against the encroachment of Chaos, they were unable to escape their inevitable doom, and within five hundred years of the Fall their craftworld was swallowed into the warp. Not a soul escaped its clutches but for the Phoenix Lord known as Maugan Ra, the Harvester of Souls, most mighty Exarch of the Shrine of the Dark Reapers.

When Asurmen taught his brethren the arts of war it was Maugan Ra that fell furthest from the fold. He fashioned baroque weapons of occult nature; not the blades of his brethren but dark and malefic artefacts that could slay his foes from afar. As his craft progressed, Maugan Ra learnt that even the mightiest weapon could be used with the precision of a scalpel. This led to the creation of the Maugetar, also known as the Harvester, and later to the disciplines of the Dark Reaper aspect itself.

Aspect: Dark Reapers

Wargear: The Maugetar. This is an ancient shuriken cannon that has an inbuilt executioner (see page 23). It has the following profile:

Range: 36"   S: 6   AP: 5   Assault 4, Pinning, Rending

Warrior Powers: Maugan Ra has the Crack Shot and Fast Shot Exarch powers.

Acute Senses: Maugan Ra can pick out a well-hidden foe even in the dark of a moonlit night. He has the Acute Senses special rule.

THE GHOSTS OF ALTANSAR

Ten thousand years after the Eye of Terror swallowed Maugan Ra's homeworld, Abaddon the Despoiler launched his thirteenth Black Crusade from within its depths. The nightmarish realm vomited the legions of Chaos into the material universe, leaving a gaping rift between the material universe and that of the Warp. Whilst the Eye was still open, Maugan Ra undertook a perilous quest into its malignant reaches in search of the remains of his people. Leaving a silvered trail of soulfire behind him, Maugan Ra eventually found the remains of his craftworld. The Eldar of Altansar lived on still, after a fashion.

Maugan Ra guided what was left of his craftworld out of the Eye of Terror, and led them against the forces of the Despoiler to deny him ultimate victory. However, there was no celebration, no welcome from the other craftworlds. The shadowy Eldar of Altansar are treated with open suspicion and hostility, for how could any Eldar remain untouched by the predations of Chaos for so many millenia?

ELDAR ARMY LIST

The following pages contain an army list that enables you to field an Eldar army and fight battles using the scenarios included in the Warhammer 40,000 rulebook. It also provides you with the basic information you'll need in order to field an Eldar army in scenarios you've devised yourself, or that form part of a campaign.

The army list is split into five sections. All the squads, vehicles and characters in the army are placed into one of these depending upon their role on the battlefield. Each model is also given a points value, which varies depending on how effective that model is in battle. Before you choose an army, you will need to agree with your opponent upon a scenario and the total number of points each of you will spend. Then you can proceed to pick your army as described below.

> "War is my master; Death my mistress."
>
> **Maugan Ra**

USING A FORCE ORGANISATION CHART

The army lists are used in conjunction with the force organisation chart from a scenario. Each chart is split into five categories that correspond to the sections in the army list, and each category has one or more boxes. Each box indicates that you may make one choice from that section of the army list, while a dark-toned box means that you must make a choice from that section. Note that unless a model or vehicle forms part of a squad or a squadron, it is a single choice from what is available to your army.

USING THE ARMY LISTS

To make a choice, look in the relevant section of the army list and decide what unit you want to have in your army, how many models there will be in it, and which upgrades you want (if any). Remember that you cannot field models that are equipped with weapons or wargear not shown on the model. Once this is done subtract the points value of the unit from your total points, and then go back and make another choice. Continue doing this until you have spent all your points. Then you're ready to do battle!

ARMY LIST ENTRIES

Each army list entry consists of the following:

Unit Name: The type of unit, which may also show a limitation on the maximum number of choices you can make of that unit type.

Profile: These are the characteristics of that unit type, including its points cost. Where the unit has different warriors, there may be more than one profile.

Number/Squad: This shows the number of models in the unit, or the number of models you may take for one choice from the force organisation chart. Often this is a variable amount, in which case it shows the minimum and maximum unit size.

Weapons: These are the unit's standard weapons.

Options: This lists the different weapon and equipment options for the unit and any additional points for taking these options. It may also include an option to upgrade the squad to include a character.

Special Rules: This is where you'll find any special rules that apply to the unit. See the Forces of the Eldar section for the details of these rules.

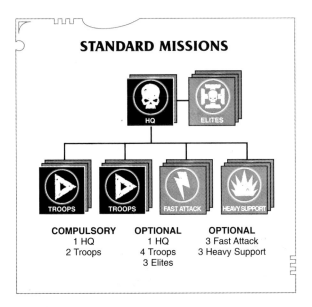

STANDARD MISSIONS

COMPULSORY	OPTIONAL	OPTIONAL
1 HQ	1 HQ	3 Fast Attack
2 Troops	4 Troops	3 Heavy Support
	3 Elites	

> "It is all too easy for an Eldar to embrace the obscene virtues of Chaos, for Slaanesh is nothing more than a manifestation of the Eldar mind in its most wild and unconstrained form. Human morality is meaningless to the Eldar, and to the dark side of the Eldar mind all life is to be expended at a whim. Cruelty and generosity are but the impulse of a moment. Beauty and sensuality are virtues that can be expressed in bloodshed just as easily as in song. To an unfettered Eldar mind there is neither sanity nor madness, but merely a wave of perfect existence fulfilled by its own savage momentum."
>
> **Ralamine Mung,**
> **Ordo Xenos**

 HQ

⚜ AUTARCH — 70 points

	WS	BS	S	T	W	I	A	Ld	Sv
Autarch	6	6	3	3	3	6	3	10	3+

Unit Type: Infantry (or Jetbike if mounted on a jetbike, or Jump Infantry if equipped with a Warp Spider jump generator or Swooping Hawks wings).

Wargear: Shuriken pistol, plasma grenades, haywire grenades, forceshield (4+ invulnerable save).

Special Rules
Independent Character, Fleet of Foot, Master Strategist.

Options
An Autarch may also be given one of the following:
Swooping Hawk wings . . . . 20 points
Warp jump generator . . . . 25 points
Eldar jetbike. 30 points

An Autarch may also be given one of the following:
Banshee mask. 3 points
Mandiblasters . . . . 10 points

An Autarch may be given one single-handed weapon and one two-handed weapon:
Single-handed weapons
Power weapon . . . . 10 points
Scorpion chainsword . . . . 5 points
Laser lance (only on jetbike) . . . . 20 points

Two-handed weapons
Avenger shuriken catapult . . . . 2 points
Death spinner . . . . 5 points
Fusion gun . . . . 10 points
Lasblaster . . . . 1 point
Reaper launcher . . . . 25 points

⚜ FARSEER — 55 points

	WS	BS	S	T	W	I	A	Ld	Sv
Farseer	5	5	3	3	3	5	1	10	–

Unit Type: Infantry (or Jetbike if mounted on a jetbike).

Wargear: Ghosthelm, shuriken pistol, witchblade and rune armour (4+ invulnerable save).

Special Rules: Independent Character, Fleet of Foot, Psychic Powers.

Warlocks: For each Farseer in the army, you may include a squad of 3-10 Warlocks (see entry below). This unit and the Farseer are a single HQ choice.

Options: A Farseer may be given any of the following:
Upgrade witchblade to singing spear . . . . . . 3 points
Runes of warding . . . . 15 points
Runes of witnessing . . . . 10 points
Spirit stones . . . . 20 points
Eldar jetbike. 30 points

A Farseer must buy between one and four Farseer Psychic powers from the following list:
Doom . . . . 25 points
Eldritch Storm . . . . 20 points
Fortune . . . . 30 points
Guide . . . . 20 points
Mind War. . . . . 20 points

⚜ WARLOCKS — 25 points/model

	WS	BS	S	T	W	I	A	Ld	Sv
Warlock	4	4	3	3	1	4	1	8	–

Squad: 3 to 10 Warlocks.

Unit Type: Infantry (or Jetbike if riding Eldar jetbikes).

Wargear: Rune armour (4+ invulnerable save), shuriken pistol and witchblade.

Special Rules: Warlock Powers, Fleet of Foot, Spiritseers.

Transport: If not riding jetbikes, a Warlock unit may be mounted in a Wave Serpent (see entry).

Options: All Warlocks may buy one Warlock psychic power from the following list:
Conceal . . . . 15 points
Destructor . . . . 10 points
Embolden . . . . 5 points
Enhance . . . . 15 points

All Warlocks may choose from the following:
Upgrade to Spiritseer . . . . 6 points
Upgrade witchblade to singing spear . . . 3 points
Mount all Warlocks in the
unit on Eldar jetbikes . . . . . . 20 points/model

THE AVATAR OF KHAINE   155 points

	WS	BS	S	T	W	I	A	Ld	Sv
Avatar	10	5	6	6	4	6	4	10	3+

Individual: An army can only include one Avatar.

Unit Type: Monstrous Creature.

Wargear: The Wailing Doom

Special Rules: Daemon (4+ invulnerable save); Fearless; Molten Body; Inspiring; Monstrous Creature.

PRINCE YRIEL OF IYANDEN   155 points

	WS	BS	S	T	W	I	A	Ld	Sv
Prince Yriel	6	6	3	3	3	7	4	10	3+

Individual: An army can only include one Yriel.

Unit Type: Infantry.

Wargear: Forceshield (4+ invulnerable save), the Eye of Wrath, the Spear of Twilight, plasma grenades.

Special Rules: Independent Character; Master Strategist; Fleet of Foot; Doomed.

ELDRAD ULTHRAN   210 points

	WS	BS	S	T	W	I	A	Ld	Sv
Eldrad	5	5	3	4	3	5	1	10	–

Individual: An army can only include one Eldrad.

Unit Type: Infantry.

Wargear: Shuriken pistol, Staff of Ulthamar, runes of warding, runes of witnessing, ghosthelm, spirit stones, witchblade, rune armour (3+ invulnerable save).

Psychic Powers: Eldritch Storm, Fortune, Guide, Doom, and Mind War.

Special Rules: Independent Character; Divination.

Warlocks: Eldrad counts as a Farseer for the purposes of including a Warlock unit.

PHOENIX LORD   cost varies, see below

	WS	BS	S	T	W	I	A	Ld	Sv
Phoenix Lord	7	7	4	4	3	7	4	10	2+

Unit Type: Infantry (Baharroth is Jump Infantry).

Individual: An army can only include one of each Phoenix Lord.

ASURMEN   230 points
Wargear: Wrist-mounted Avenger shuriken catapults, the Sword of Asur.

Special Rules: Independent Character; Fleet of Foot; Fearless; Eternal Warriors; Disciples (Dire Avengers); Defend; Bladestorm; Battle Fate (4+ invulnerable save).

JAIN ZAR   190 points
Wargear: Banshee mask, executioner, the Silent Death.

Special Rules: Independent Character; Fleet of Foot; Fearless; Eternal Warriors; Disciples (Howling Banshees); Acrobatic; War Shout; Furious Charge.

BAHARROTH   200 points
Wargear: Swooping Hawk wings, Swooping Hawk grenade pack, plasma grenades, haywire grenades, power weapon, hawk's talon.

Special Rules: Independent Character; Fleet of Foot; Fearless; Eternal Warriors; Disciples (Swooping Hawks); Skyleap; Intercept; Hit and Run.

KARANDRAS   215 points
Wargear: The Scorpion's Bite, scorpion chainsword, scorpion's claw, plasma grenades.

Special Rules: Independent Character; Fleet of Foot; Fearless; Eternal Warriors; Disciples (Striking Scorpions); Shadowstrike; Stalker; Stealth.

FUEGAN   205 points
Wargear: Firepike, the Fire Axe, melta bombs.

Special Rules: Independent Character; Fleet of Foot; Fearless; Eternal Warriors; Disciples (Fire Dragons); Tank Hunter; Crack Shot; Feel No Pain.

MAUGAN RA   195 points
Wargear: The Maugetar.

Special Rules: Independent Character; Fleet of Foot; Fearless; Eternal Warriors; Disciples (Dark Reapers); Crack Shot; Fast Shot; Acute Senses.

✠ ELITES ✠

☗ STRIKING SCORPIONS   16 points/model

	WS	BS	S	T	W	I	A	Ld	Sv
Striking Scorpion	4	4	3	3	1	5	1	9	3+
Exarch	5	5	3	3	1	6	2	9	3+

Squad: 5 to 10 Striking Scorpions.

Unit Type: Infantry.

Wargear: Shuriken pistol, scorpion chainsword, mandiblaster and plasma grenades.

Character: One model in the squad may be upgraded to an Exarch at an additional cost of +12 points. The Exarch may replace his shuriken pistol with a scorpion's claw at +15 points, replace his chainsword with a biting blade at +5 points, or replace both with chainsabres at +5 points.

The Exarch may be given the following warrior powers: Stalker at +5 points; Shadowstrike at +20 points.

Transport: The Striking Scorpions may be mounted in a Wave Serpent (see entry).

☖ FIRE DRAGONS   16 points/model

	WS	BS	S	T	W	I	A	Ld	Sv
Fire Dragon	4	4	3	3	1	5	1	9	4+
Exarch	5	5	3	3	1	6	2	9	3+

Squad: 5 to 10 Fire Dragons.

Unit Type: Infantry.

Wargear: Fusion gun and melta bombs.

Special Rules: Fleet of Foot.

Character: One model in the squad may be upgraded to an Exarch for +12 points. The Exarch may exchange his fusion gun for a firepike for +8 points, or a dragon's breath flamer for free.

The Exarch may be given the following warrior powers: Crack Shot for +5 points; Tank Hunters for +15 points.

Transport: The Fire Dragons may be mounted in a Wave Serpent (see entry).

☗ WRAITHGUARD   35 points/model

	WS	BS	S	T	W	I	A	Ld	Sv
Wraithguard	4	4	5	6	1	4	1	10	3+
Warlock	4	4	3	3	1	4	1	8	4+

Squad: 3 to 10 Wraithguard. A unit of 10 Wraithguard led by a Spiritseer may be fielded as either an Elites choice or a Troops choice.

Unit Type: Infantry.

Wargear: Wraithcannon.

Special Rules: Fearless, Wraithsight

Character: The unit may be accompanied by a single Warlock at +25 points. See the entry in the HQ section of the army list for his wargear and options.

Transport: A unit of up to 5 Wraithguard and 1 Warlock may be mounted in a Wave Serpent (see entry).

⚑ HOWLING BANSHEES

16 points/model

	WS	BS	S	T	W	I	A	Ld	Sv
Howling Banshee	4	4	3	3	1	5	1	9	4+
Exarch	5	5	3	3	1	6	2	9	3+

Squad: 5 to 10 Howling Banshees.

Unit Type: Infantry.

Wargear: Banshee mask, shuriken pistol and power weapon.

Special Rules: Fleet of Foot.

Character: One model in the squad may be upgraded to an Exarch for +12 points. The Exarch may replace her power weapon with an executioner at +10 points or a triskele at +5 points. Alternatively she may replace her power weapon and shuriken pistol with mirrorswords at +10 points.

The Exarch may be given the following warrior powers: War Shout at +5 points, Acrobatic at +5 points.

Transport: The Howling Banshees may be mounted in a Wave Serpent (see entry).

✸ HARLEQUIN TROUPE

18 points/model

	WS	BS	S	T	W	I	A	Ld	Sv
Harlequin	5	4	3	3	1	6	2	9	–
Shadowseer	5	4	3	3	1	6	2	9	–
Death Jester	5	4	3	3	1	6	2	9	–
Troupe Master	5	4	3	3	1	6	3	10	–

Squad: 5 to 10 Harlequins.

Unit Type: Infantry.

Wargear: Shuriken pistol, close combat weapon, flip belts & holo-suits (5+ invulnerable save).

Special Rules: Dance of Death, Fleet of Foot.

Options: Any model may exchange its close combat weapon for a Harlequin's Kiss at +4 points per model. Up to two models may exchange their shuriken pistol for a fusion pistol for +10 points per model.

Character: One Harlequin may be upgraded to a Troupe Master for +20 points, replacing his close combat weapon with either a power weapon or a Harlequin's Kiss for free. One Harlequin may be upgraded to a Death Jester for +10 points, replacing his weapons with a shrieker cannon. One Harlequin may be upgraded to a Shadowseer for +30 points.

TRANSPORT

☒ WAVE SERPENT

90 points/model

	Front Armour	Side Armour	Rear Armour	BS
Wave Serpent	12	12	10	3

Type: Skimmer, Tank, Fast.

Wargear: Twin-linked shuriken catapults and one weapon from the following list: twin-linked shuriken cannons at +10 points; twin-linked scatter lasers at +25 points; twin-linked Eldar missile launchers at +30 points; twin-linked starcannons at +35 points; twin-linked bright lances at +45 points.

Special Rules: Energy Field.

Options: The twin-linked shuriken catapults may be upgraded to a single shuriken cannon for +10 points.

Wave Serpents may be upgraded with vectored engines at +20 points, star engines at +15 points and spirit stones at +10 points.

Transport: The Serpent is a dedicated transport that can carry a single unit of infantry of up to 12 models. Wraithguard, however, are somewhat larger, and so only 5 Wraithguard models and up to two accompanying characters can be transported.

◄ TROOPS ►

⚤ DIRE AVENGERS

12 points/model

	WS	BS	S	T	W	I	A	Ld	Sv
Dire Avenger	4	4	3	3	1	5	1	9	4+
Exarch	5	5	3	3	1	6	2	9	3+

Squad: 5 to 10 Dire Avengers.

Unit Type: Infantry.

Wargear: Avenger shuriken catapult.

Special Rules: Fleet of Foot.

Character: One model in the squad may be upgraded to an Exarch for +12 points. The Exarch may replace his shuriken catapult with two shuriken catapults at +5 points (counting as a single Assault 4 Avenger shuriken catapult); with a diresword and shuriken pistol at +10 points, or with a power weapon and shimmershield at +15 points.

The Exarch may be given the following Exarch powers: Defend for +15 points; Bladestorm for +15 points.

Transport: The Dire Avengers may be mounted in a Wave Serpent (see entry).

⚥ RANGERS

19 points/model

	WS	BS	S	T	W	I	A	Ld	Sv
Ranger	3	4	3	3	1	4	1	8	5+

Squad: 5 to 10 Rangers.

Unit Type: Infantry.

Wargear: Ranger long rifle, shuriken pistol.

Special Rules: Fleet of Foot, Masters of Stealth, Pathfinders

Options: Any squad of Rangers can be upgraded to Pathfinders at the cost of +5 points per model.

⚤ GUARDIANS

8 points/model

	WS	BS	S	T	W	I	A	Ld	Sv
Guardian	3	3	3	3	1	4	1	8	5+
Warlock	4	4	3	3	1	4	1	8	4+

Squad: 10 to 20 Guardians.

Unit Type: Infantry.

Wargear: Shuriken catapult.

Special Rules: Fleet of Foot.

Character: The unit may be accompanied by a single Warlock at +25 points. See the entry in the HQ section of the army list for his wargear and options.

Options: Two Guardians must be upgraded to a weapon team with a heavy weapon platform, chosen from the following list: bright lance +30 points; Eldar missile launcher +20 points; scatter laser +15 points; shuriken cannon +5 points; starcannon +25 points.

Storm Guardians. Any squad of Guardians may be upgraded to Storm Guardians. In this case they exchange their shuriken catapults for shuriken pistols and close combat weapons at no additional cost. They do not have a heavy weapon platform, but up to two models in the squad may exchange their weapons for either a fusion gun at +6 points per model or a flamer at +6 points per model.

Transport: A Guardian squad including 12 models or less may be mounted in a Wave Serpent (see entry).

⚤ GUARDIAN JETBIKE SQUADRON

22 points/model

	WS	BS	S	T	W	I	A	Ld	Sv
Guardian Jetbike	3	3	3	3(4)	1	4	1	8	3+
Warlock	4	4	3	3(4)	1	4	1	8	3+

Squad: 3 to 12 Guardian Jetbikes.

Unit Type: Jetbikes.

Wargear: Twin-linked shuriken catapults.

Options: Every third Guardian Jetbike may replace its shuriken catapults with a single shuriken cannon at +10 points per model.

Character: The unit may be accompanied by a single jetbike-mounted Warlock at +45 points. See the entry in the HQ section for his wargear and options.

⚡ FAST ATTACK ⚡

✠ SHINING SPEARS

35 points/model

	WS	BS	S	T	W	I	A	Ld	Sv
Shining Spear	4	4	3	3(4)	1	5	1	9	3+
Exarch	5	5	3	3(4)	1	6	2	9	3+

Squad: 3 to 5 Shining Spears.

Unit Type: Jetbikes.

Wargear: The jetbikes are armed with twin-linked shuriken catapults. The riders carry laser lances.

Character: One model in the squad may be upgraded to an Exarch for +12 points. He may replace his twin-linked shuriken catapults with a single shuriken cannon at +15 points. The Exarch may replace his laser lance with a power weapon for free, or a star lance at +15 points.

The Exarch may be given the following warrior powers: Skilled Rider for +10 points, Withdraw for +25 points.

✠ WARP SPIDERS

22 points/model

	WS	BS	S	T	W	I	A	Ld	Sv
Warp Spider	4	4	3	3	1	5	1	9	3+
Exarch	5	5	3	3	1	6	2	9	3+

Squad: 5 to 10 Warp Spiders.

Unit Type: Jump Infantry.

Wargear: Death spinner.

Character: One model in the squad may be upgraded to an Exarch for +12 points. The Exarch may be armed with an additional death spinner for +5 points (making his death spinner an Assault 4 weapon), or replace his death spinner with a spinneret rifle at +5 points. The Exarch may also be equipped with powerblades at +10 points.

The Exarch may have the following warrior powers: Surprise Assault at +10 points; Withdraw at +15 points.

✠ SWOOPING HAWKS

21 points/model

	WS	BS	S	T	W	I	A	Ld	Sv
Swooping Hawk	4	4	3	3	1	5	1	9	4+
Exarch	5	5	3	3	1	6	2	9	3+

Squad: 5 to 10 Swooping Hawks.

Unit Type: Jump Infantry.

Wargear: Lasblaster, plasma grenades, haywire grenades, Swooping Hawk grenade pack.

Special Rules: Fleet of Foot.

Character: One model in the squad may be upgraded to an Exarch for +12 points. The Exarch may be armed with a power weapon for +10 points or replace his lasblaster for a hawk's talon for +10 points or a sunrifle at +15 points.

The Exarch may be given the following warrior powers: Skyleap for +15 points, Intercept at +5 points.

✠ VYPER SQUADRON

45 points/model

	Front Armour	Side Armour	Rear Armour	BS
Vyper	10	10	10	3

Squadron: 1-3 Vypers.

Type: Fast, Skimmer, Open-topped.

Wargear: The Vyper is armed with twin-linked shuriken catapults and a single weapon chosen from the following list: Eldar missile launcher at +20 points; scatter laser at +15 points; starcannon at +25 points; shuriken cannon at +5 points; bright lance at +30 points.

Options: The shuriken catapults can be upgraded to a single shuriken cannon for +10 points.

Each Vyper may be upgraded with vectored engines at +20 points, star engines at +15 points, holo-fields at +35 points and spirit stones at +10 points.

HEAVY SUPPORT

SUPPORT WEAPON BATTERY — 20 points/weapon

	WS	BS	S	T	W	I	A	Ld	Sv
Guardian	3	3	3	3	1	4	1	8	5+
Warlock	4	4	3	3	1	4	1	8	4+

Battery: 1 to 3 support weapons (including two Guardian crew per weapon).

Unit Type: Artillery.

Wargear: All of the support weapons must be armed with the same type of weapon from the following list: D-cannon at +30 points per model; vibro cannon at +30 points per model; shadow weaver at +10 points per model.

Crew: Two Guardians armed with shuriken catapults.

Character: The unit may be accompanied by a single Warlock at +25 points. See the entry in the HQ section of the army list for his wargear and options.

DARK REAPERS — 35 points/model

	WS	BS	S	T	W	I	A	Ld	Sv
	4	4	3	3	1	5	1	9	3+
Exarch	5	5	3	3	1	6	2	9	3+

Squad: 3 to 5 Dark Reapers.

Unit Type: Infantry.

Wargear: Reaper launcher.

Character: One model in the squad may be upgraded to an Exarch for +12 points. The Exarch may replace his reaper launcher with one of the following weapons: shuriken cannon for free; Eldar missile launcher at +10 points, tempest launcher at +20 points.

The Exarch may be given the following warrior powers: Fast Shot for +20 points; Crack Shot for +10 points.

Transport: A Dark Reaper squad may be mounted in a Wave Serpent (see entry).

WRAITHLORD — 90 points

	WS	BS	S	T	W	I	A	Ld	Sv
Wraithlord	4	4	10	8	3	4	2	10	3+

Unit Type: Monstrous Creature.

Wargear: The Wraithlord is armed with one shuriken catapult and a flamer, or with two shuriken catapults, or with two flamers.

In addition, it **must** be equipped with one of the following: starcannon at +30 points; bright lance at +40 points, scatter laser at +20 points; shuriken cannon at +10 points; Eldar missile launcher at +25 points; wraithsword at +10 points.

Special Rules: Fearless, Monstrous Creature, Wraithsight.

Options: The Wraithlord may choose a second weapon from the following: starcannon at +30 points; bright lance at +40 points; scatter laser at +20 points; shuriken cannon at +10 points; Eldar missile launcher at +25 points. If a duplicate weapon is chosen then they count as a single twin-linked weapon.

WAR WALKER SQUADRON — 30 points/model

	WS	BS	S	Front Armour	Side Armour	Rear Armour	I	A
War Walker	3	3	5	10	10	10	4	2

Number: 1 to 3 War Walkers.

Type: Walker.

Special Rules: Scouts.

Options: The War Walker is armed with two weapons chosen from the following list: starcannon at +25 points; Eldar missile launcher at +20 points; scatter laser at +15 points; shuriken cannon at +5 points; bright lance at +30 points.

The entire squadron can be upgraded with spirit stones at +5 points per model.

FALCON   115 points

	Front Armour	Side Armour	Rear Armour	BS
Falcon	12	12	10	3

Type: Skimmer, Tank, Fast.

Wargear: Twin-linked shuriken catapults, pulse laser and one weapon from the following list: shuriken cannon at +5 points; scatter laser at +15 points; Eldar missile launcher at +20 points; starcannon at +25 points, bright lance at +30 points.

Options: The shuriken catapults can be upgraded to a single shuriken cannon for +10 points.

Falcons may be upgraded with vectored engines at +20 points, star engines at +15 points, holo-fields at +35 points and spirit stones at +10 points.

Transport: The Falcon can carry a single unit of infantry of up to 6 models. It may not carry a Wraithguard unit.

FIRE PRISM   115 points

	Front Armour	Side Armour	Rear Armour	BS
Fire Prism	12	12	10	4

Type: Skimmer, Tank, Fast.

Wargear: Prism cannon & twin-linked shuriken catapults.

Options: The shuriken catapults can be upgraded to a single shuriken cannon for +10 points.

Fire Prisms may be upgraded with vectored engines at +20 points, star engines at +15 points, holo-fields at +35 points and spirit stones at +10 points.

REFERENCE

TROOP TYPES

	WS	BS	S	T	W	I	A	Ld	Sv	Page
Autarch	6	6	3	3	3	6	3	10	3+	29
Avatar	10	5	6	6	4	6	4	10	3+	24
Dark Reaper	4	4	3	3	1	5	1	9	3+	34
Death Jester	5	4	3	3	1	6	2	9	–	48
Dire Avenger	4	4	3	3	1	5	1	9	4+	30
Eldrad Ulthran	5	5	3	4	3	5	1	10	–	50
Exarch	5	5	3	3	1	6	2	9	3+	*
Farseer	5	5	3	3	3	5	1	10	–	26
Fire Dragon	4	4	3	3	1	5	1	9	4+	32
Guardian	3	3	3	3	1	4	1	8	5+	39
Guardian Jetbike	3	3	3	3(4)	1	4	1	8	3+	40
Harlequin	5	4	3	3	1	6	2	9	–	48
Howling Banshee	4	4	3	3	1	5	1	9	4+	31
Phoenix Lord	7	7	4	4	3	7	4	10	2+	54
Ranger	3	4	3	3	1	4	1	8	5+	38
Shadowseer	5	4	3	3	1	6	2	9	–	48
Shining Spear	4	4	3	3(4)	1	5	1	9	3+	37
Striking Scorpion	4	4	3	3	1	5	1	9	3+	33
Swooping Hawk	4	4	3	3	1	5	1	9	4+	35
Troupe Master	5	4	3	3	1	6	3	10	–	48
Warlock	4	4	3	3	1	4	1	8	–	27
Warp Spider	4	4	3	3	1	5	1	9	3+	36
Wraithguard	4	4	5	6	1	4	1	10	3+	46
Wraithlord	4	4	10	8	3	4	2	10	3+	47
Yriel	6	6	3	3	3	7	4	10	3+	52

Individual Exarchs can be found in their respective Aspect entries.

ELDAR VEHICLES

	WS	BS	S	Armour Front	Side	Rear	I	A	Page
War Walker	3	3	5	10	10	10	4	2	44
Wave Serpent	–	3	–	12	12	10	–	–	45
Falcon	–	3	–	12	12	10	–	–	42
Fire Prism	–	4	–	12	12	10	–	–	43
Vyper	–	3	–	10	10	10	–	–	41

RANGED WEAPONS

	Range	S	AP	Type
Avenger shuriken catapult	18"	4	5	Assault 2
Bright lance	36"	8	2	Heavy 1, Lance
D-cannon*	G24"	X	2	Heavy 1, Blast
Death spinner	12"	6	–	Assault 2
Dragon's breath flamer	Template	5	4	Assault 1
Exarch deathspinner	12"	6	–	Assault 4
Firepike	18"	8	1	Assault 1, Melta
Flamer	Template	4	5	Assault 1
Fusion gun	12"	8	1	Assault 1, Melta
Fusion pistol	6"	8	1	Pistol, Melta
Hawk's talon	24"	5	5	Assault 3
Lasblaster	24"	3	5	Assault 2
Laser lance	6"	6	4	Assault 1, Lance
Eldar missile launcher (krak)	48"	8	3	Heavy 1
Eldar missile launcher (plasma)	48"	4	4	Heavy 1, Blast, Pinning
Prism cannon (focussed)*	60"	9	2	Heavy 1, Blast
Prism cannon (dispersed)*	60"	5	4	Heavy 1, Large Blast
Pulse laser	48"	8	2	Heavy 2
Ranger long rifle*	36"	X	6	Heavy 1, Sniper, Pinning
Reaper launcher	48"	5	3	Heavy 2
Scatter laser	36"	6	6	Heavy 4
Singing spear*	12"	X	6	Assault 1
Shadow weaver	G48"	6	–	Heavy 1, Blast
Shrieker cannon	24"	6	5	Assault 3, Pinning
Shuriken cannon	24"	6	5	Assault 3
Shuriken catapult	12"	4	5	Assault 2
Shuriken pistol	12"	4	5	Pistol
Spinneret rifle	18"	6	1	Assault 1, Pinning
Star lance	6"	8	4	Assault 1, Lance
Starcannon	36"	6	2	Heavy 2
Sunrifle	24"	3	5	Assault 6, Pinning
Tempest launcher	G36"	4	3	Heavy 2, Blast
Triskele	12"	3	2	Assault 3
Vibro cannon*	36"	4	–	Heavy 1, Pinning
Wraithcannon*	12"	X	2	Assault 1

These weapons have additional rules. See the Weapons section of the Warhammer 40,000 rulebook or the Forces of the Eldar section.

Original Book
Rick Priestley

Cover Art
Paul Dainton

Illustration
John Blanche, Alex Boyd, Roberto Cirillo,
Paul Dainton, David Gallagher,
Mark Gibbons, Jes Goodwin, Des Hanley,
Karl Kopinski, Paul Smith, Geoff Taylor
& Richard Wright

Graphic Design
Pete Borlace & Alun Davies

Miniatures Design
Tim Adcock, Juan Diaz, Martin Footitt,
Jes Goodwin & Mark Harrison

Hobby Material
Dave Andrews, Neil Hodgson,
Mark Jones, Chad Mierzwa,
Dominic Murray & Adrian Wood

'Eavy Metal
Fil Dunn, Pete Foley, Neil Green,
Neil Langdown, Darren Latham,
Keith Robertson, Anja Wettergren
& Kirsten Williams

Production
Michelle Barson, Jon Cave,
Marc Elliott, Dylan Owen, Mark Owen,
Ian Strickland & Nathan Winter

Special thanks to
*Gav Thorpe, Alessio Cavatore,
Graham Davey, Paul Gayner,
Alan Merrett, Rick Priestley,
Adam Richardson, Jeremy Vetock
& The Ancient and Honourable
Order of Techpriests*

UK
Games Workshop Ltd.,
Willow Rd, Lenton,
Nottingham,
NG7 2WS

US
Games Workshop Inc.,
6711 Baymeadow Drive,
Glen Burnie,
Maryland 21060-6401

Canada
Games Workshop,
2679 Bristol Circle,
Unit 3, Oakville,
Ontario, L6H 6Z8

Australia
Games Workshop,
23 Liverpool Street,
Ingleburn
NSW 2565

THE ELDAR WARHOST

Each Eldar craftworld has its own signature colour scheme. However, the Aspect Warriors and certain other units have their own traditional colours that are not dependent upon the craftworld from which they come. Players building an Eldar force must decide which craftworld their force will originate from (or invent one!), as well as which mix of specialised units to select. This section shows painted examples of characters, squads, vehicles and complete armies, as well as the colour schemes for the major craftworlds.

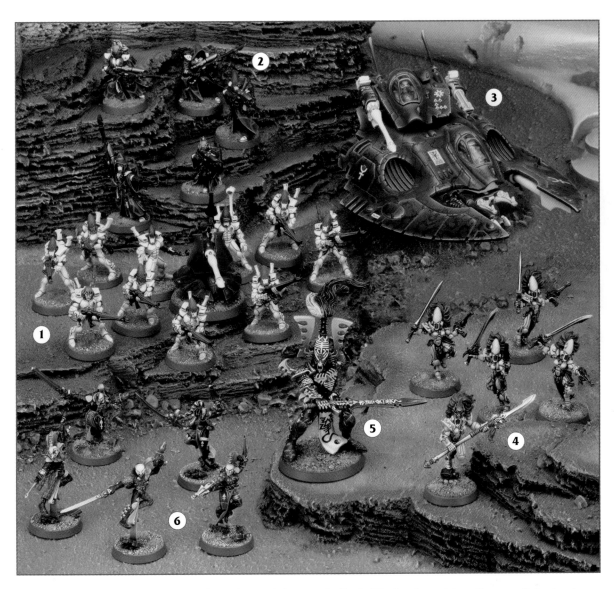

1. The Guardians' uniforms display the colours of the Biel-Tan craftworld. The colour schemes for the various craftworlds are presented on the following pages.

2. The armoured suits of this Ranger squad show the Biel-Tan colours, although these are partially covered by their camo-cloaks.

3. The vehicles of the craftworld use the same green and white, as well as displaying the craftworld's rune.

4. Each Warrior Aspect has its own distinct colours, following the traditions of their individual shrines. These are detailed on pages 79-81.

5. The fearsome Avatar is the colour of molten metal, covered in glowing runes.

6. Harlequins don't have a uniform as such – their holosuits display a myriad of colours and patterns, confusing to the eyes of their enemies.

BIEL-TAN

Rune armour

Singing spear

Farseer
with singing spear

Helmet with
mandiblasters

Warp jump generator
(showing runic heirogram)

Autarch with scorpion
chainsword and shuriken pistol

A Warlock leads a squad of Guardians, supported by a War Walker and a Wraithlord.

BIEL-TAN COLOUR SCHEME

Biel-Tan uses a white and green colour scheme, often with the addition of their distinctive thorn pattern.

○ Skull White

● Snot Green

 Craftworld rune

Guardian

Scatter laser weapon platform

PAINTING THORNS

The thorn pattern of Biel-Tan is simple to achieve:

1. Mark out a thin, curved line.

2. Thicken the line to the desired width.

3. Add on the pointed thorns.

Eldar missile launcher

Starcannon

Shuriken cannon

Bright lance

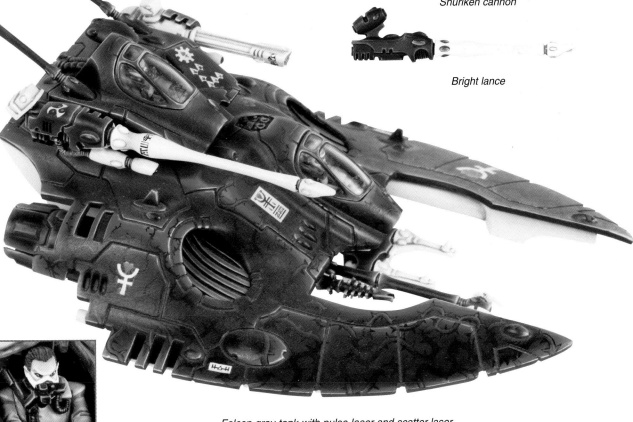

Falcon grav-tank with pulse laser and scatter laser

SAIM-HANN

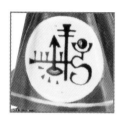

Autarch with power weapon
and shuriken pistol

Force shield

Farseer with witchblade

Ranger

Warlock with singing spear

Warlock with witchblade

A Wave Serpent and two Vypers support a squadron of Guardian Jetbikes.

Guardian

D-cannon

Vibro-cannon support weapon

Wraithlord with shuriken catapults, wraithsword and bright lance

HOBBY TIP

Don't glue on the clear canopies until you have painted the cockpit (and applied any spray varnish).

ULTHWÉ

Eldrad Ulthran

Farseer rune

Farseer with shuriken pistol

The Ulthwé
craftworld rune

ULTHWÉ COLOUR SCHEME

The troops and vehicles
of the Ulthwé craftworld
are mostly black, with
bone coloured
decoration.

● Chaos Black

○ Bleached Bone

 Craftworld rune

Guardian

Warlock with witchblade

Warlock with witchblade
and shuriken pistol

Fire Prism

IYANDEN

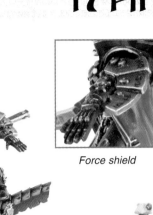

Prince Yriel

Force shield

Guardian

Shadow Weaver support weapon

A Wraithlord and Wraithguard guided by a Spiritseer.

Autarch with power weapon,
shuriken pistol,
Banshee mask and
Swooping Hawk wings

Force shield

War Walker with two scatter lasers

Ranger

Ranger

Ranger

PAINTING GEMSTONES

Gemstones can simply be painted a flat colour and given a coat of gloss varnish. Alternatively you could try one of the three colour schemes and the steps shown here:

	1	**2**	**3**	**4**
Red gems:	● Blood Red	● Blazing Orange	● Fiery Orange	○ Skull White
Green gems:	● Dark Angels Green	● Snot Green	● Scorpion Green	○ Skull White
Blue gems:	● Regal Blue	● Enchanted Blue	● Ice Blue	○ Skull White

Vyper with starcannon   Guardian

OTHER CRAFTWORLDS

YME-LOC

● Codex Grey

● Blazing Orange

Craftworld rune

The Eldar of Yme-Loc are talented artisans, and their armies are supported by powerful grav-tanks and Titans.

LUGGANATH

● Fiery Orange

● Chaos Black

Craftworld rune

The renegades of Lugganath foster close ties with the Harlequins, for they hope to abandon this galaxy and start civilisation afresh, claiming the webway as their realm.

ALTANSAR

● Red Gore

● Chaos Black

Craftworld rune

The Eldar of of Altansar, having recently escaped their millennia-long incarceration within the Eye of Terror, are treated with much suspicion by the other craftworlds.

IL-KAITHE

● Snot Green

● Liche Purple

Craftworld rune

The Eldar of Il-Kaithe constantly crusade against the forces of Chaos. Their talented Bonesingers are said to be able to practice their art even in the heat of battle.

IYBRAESIL

● Hawk Turquoise

○ Skull White

Craftworld rune

Iybraesil is a largely matriarchal society, and as followers of Morai-Heg they constantly aspire to recovering the hidden secrets of the crone worlds.

For a wealth of techniques and ideas about painting your models:

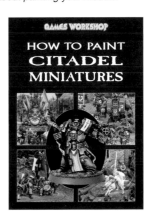

AVATAR

HARLEQUINS

Harlequin with shuriken pistol
and Harlequin's Kiss

Harlequin with fusion pistol
and combat weapon

Harlequin with shuriken
pistol and combat weapon

Harlequin with Harlequin's
Kiss and shuriken pistol

Painting Diamonds

The holosuits of the Harlequins project
intricate patterns in different colours.

*1. Draw lines to
make a grid.*

*2. Colour in the
diamond shapes.*

*3. A highlight
will add further
definition.*

Harlequin with fusion
pistol and combat weapon

Death Jester with
shrieker cannon

ASPECT WARRIORS

DIRE AVENGERS COLOUR SCHEME
- ● Regal Blue
- ○ Skull White

Dire Avenger

Dire Avenger Exarch with power weapon and shimmer shield

Asurmen

WARP SPIDERS COLOUR SCHEME
- ● Red Gore
- ○ Skull White

Warp Spider

Warp Spider Exarch with twin death spinners and powerblades

SHINING SPEARS COLOUR SCHEME
- ○ Skull White
- ● Regal Blue

Shining Spear

Shining Spear Exarch with power weapon

Swooping Hawk

Swooping Hawk Exarch
with hawk's talon

Baharroth

Howling Banshee

Howling Banshee Exarch
with executioner

Mirror swords

Jain-Zar

Missile launcher

Dark Reaper

Dark Reaper Exarch
with tempest launcher

Maugan Ra

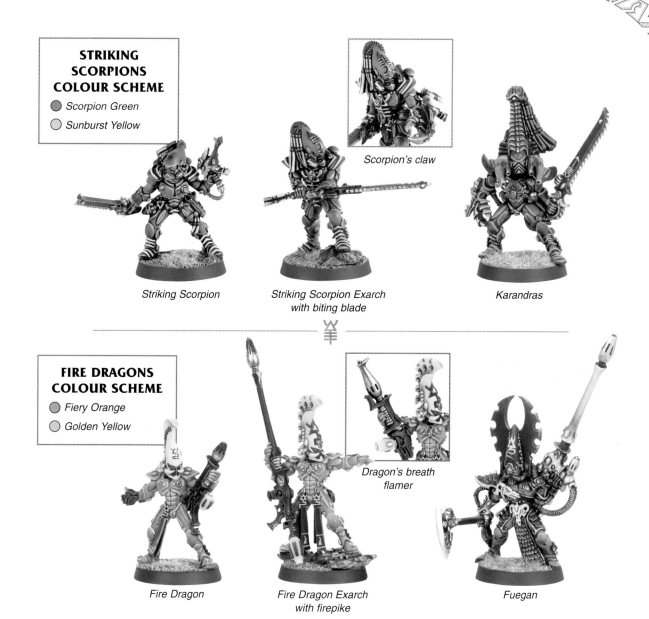

STRIKING SCORPIONS COLOUR SCHEME
- Scorpion Green
- Sunburst Yellow

Scorpion's claw

Striking Scorpion

Striking Scorpion Exarch with biting blade

Karandras

FIRE DRAGONS COLOUR SCHEME
- Fiery Orange
- Golden Yellow

Dragon's breath flamer

Fire Dragon

Fire Dragon Exarch with firepike

Fuegan

Dire Avenger squad

COLLECTING AN ELDAR FORCE

The army shown on these pages is a good example of a 1,500 point force, containing a broad selection of the units that the Eldar warhost has to offer. This is by no means the definitive Eldar army; in fact the beauty of the Eldar army is that it is customisable to suit your own styles and to combat the specific armies of your opponents. If you are new to the Eldar, this would be a great start to your collection. If not, it might just give you a few ideas for incorporating units into your own battleforce.

ELITES – 143 points
6 Striking Scorpions, including an Exarch with a scorpion's claw and the Shadowstrike Exarch skill

FAST ATTACK – 75 points
1 Vyper with a bright lance

TROOPS – 162 points
10 Dire Avengers, including an Exarch with power weapon and shimmer shield and the Bladestorm Exarch power

ELITES – 131 points
6 Fire Dragons, including an Exarch with a firepike and the Tank Hunters' Exarch skill

HQ – 133 points
Farseer with Guide, Doom, singing spear, runes of witnessing and spirit stones

HQ – 110 points
Autarch with shuriken pistol, scorpion chainsword, mandiblasters and warp jump generator

HEAVY SUPPORT – 185 points
Falcon with a pulse laser and scatter laser, plus vectored engines and holofields

TROOPS – 95 points
5 Rangers

ELITES – 187 points
10 Howling Banshees including an Exarch with an executioner and the War Shout Exarch power

TROOPS – 150 points
10 Guardians, including a starcannon platform and crew and a Warlock with Conceal, a witchblade and a shuriken pistol

HEAVY SUPPORT – 130 points
Wraithlord with bright lance